GARDENS IN GLASS CONTAINERS

GARDENS IN GLASS CONTAINERS

by

Robert C. Baur

Hearthside Press Inc.
New York

JY2 '71

CONTENTS

GARDENS IN GLASS CONTAINERS

A low-maintenance window garden includes houseplants in pots (the pots concealed by sphagnum moss lining the tank) and in hanging bottles. The plants water themselves by moisture condensation.

Foreword

TERRARIUMS TO THE FORE

Do you remember the Victorian parlor? Depending on your age, it could have been your parents' or your grandparents'—or photographs in the family album. Thanks to the plants-inside-of-glass pioneering done by Dr. Nathaniel Ward in the early 19th century, to be chronicled in our first chapter, the Victorian parlor abounded in sunshine jars, fern cases, and mantel cloches of dried everlastings.

So gardening in glass containers is not a new fad. But the pace of contemporary life, the growing preponderance of apartment-dwelling, the development of lightweight plastic containers, specially designed window greenhouses and plantariums equipped with heating cables and fluorescent lights have made this nigh-effortless, worryless, and waterless form of gardening completely contemporary and burgeoningly popular.

There's been a surfeit of books about green thumbs and gardening. And yet, because you've got the wrong exposure in your flat, or find yourself forced to leave town with no one to tend your potted greenery, you may have come a cropper in your gardening attempts thus far. It gives me pleasure to tell you, with reassuring conviction, that you do *not* need a green thumb to be a successful terrarium gardener. You'll develop a delicate thumb, I hope; one that coordinates well with your index finger. But if you plant it properly, water it as instructed and no more, and give it proper lighting exposure, your terrarium garden will require a minimum of care. Gardens in glass are green pastures indeed for working housewife, businessman, plant-lover-on-vacation, or the forgetful person. They have equal charm and utility for the seasoned gardener, too: transparent containers are fine spots for engendering seeds and cuttings, later to be transplanted to the out-of-doors or to exposed pots.

GLASS GARDENS GO ANYWHERE

Nor need they be confined to your home; they can be the sole undertaking in the entire office that thrives on neglect. No secretary was ever fired for failing to water a terrarium this week, and a glass garden can promote an atmosphere of relaxation, repose, warmth and informality as attractive to clients as to the staff.

Depending on what you select as your container and its contents, your glass-enclosed plantings will harmonize with any style of decor, period or contemporary. Also, they'll eliminate the often unsightly window-sill clutter of clay pots and plastic containers that are the bane of much indoor gardening; you can house an entire collection of plants inside of a single container.

Glass gardens are natural space-savers. You can tailor yours to accommodate the most limited area. A few square inches can be the site of an entire landscape replete with trees, flowering plants, lawns and reflecting pools. A famous German poem says, "Auch kleine Dinge können uns entzücken," ("Even tiny things can delight us!") There is something indefinably appealing about miniatures—an appeal to which we've all succumbed at one time or another. You can make a miniature inside of a pill-box. Because glass gardens thrive under artificial lights, you can fill a small bowl with plants that grow in low-intensity light, and place it under a table lamp equipped with a 40-watt bulb, with no appreciable increase in your utilities bill.

The terrarium is a garden for all seasons, a hobby for the year 'round. You can pattern your planting after tropical, desert or woodland themes. It can be as simple as a fern and a few pebbles, or as intricate as a Bonsai or Saikei formal garden setting. Given a cover of transparent glass, the sky's the limit!

In our comfortable-to-the-point-of-discomfort, overheated civilization, the moisture in most homes measures only about 25% during the winter. This dry indoor heat, which spells disaster to many houseplants, presents no perils to a garden in glass.

As to expense, your glass garden need cost no more than the cork stopper used to seal a discarded bottle containing slips from house-plants. Even if you don't grow your own, what you buy will come to appreciably less than what's needed for other gardening projects because it's smaller. And the tools and equipment required are mostly items you've got around the house already.

THE MULTIPURPOSE TERRARIUM

The list of glass-garden advantages goes on: one or another varia-tion of the terrarium principle can solve your Christmas and other gift problems. You can always find a ready market for your creations, and the more skillful and inventive you become, the wider the possi-bilities: bottle gardens and berry bowls are certain best-sellers at fund-raising events.

Moreover, you can become a self-made florist by forcing budded deciduous twigs, violets, violas, lily-of-the-valley pips, etc. during the winter months.

Nor need you restrict yourself to plant life. Close relatives of the terrarium are the aquarium and the vivarium. Small aquatic pets such as turtles, salamanders, horned toads, snakes (don't recoil!), and even crickets will lead happier lives if you provide them with a natural garden setting for a home, replete with ins and outs and hiding places.

The use of transparent covered containers can increase your gar-dening versatility enormously: try growing your own houseplants from seed. You'll be able to nurture varieties that are ordinarily unavailable, such as palms, African violets, orchids and fern spores; they are all easily launched in terrariums. And you can jump the seasonal gun, getting your annual flower and vegetable seedlings off to an early indoor start, then extending protective coverage to trans-plants by using "hotkaps" and "in-the-row plastic greenhouses." (See chapter 7.) Cuttings root quickly in moist humidity, and cool rooting terrariums will give your pots of spring-flowering bulbs an advan-tageous headstart.

Gastronomy, too, is part of the glass gardening scene: this versatile hobby can yield you a tasty harvest of mushrooms, pepper-grass, spicy cress, and onion sprouts for salad and seasonings.

Do these claims sound extravagant? I recommend the following tests and treatment for seed: (1) Place the contents of your leftover seed packets in plastic boxes filled with moist moss. See what happens. (2) Spread your late-ripening seeds in layers (the formal term is "stratify"), refrigerate in moss-filled jars. (3) Store others, in fact all kinds of seed, for as long a period as you like, in dry airtight bottles such as glass-stoppered apothecary jars. Their viability is assured. (See sections on "Stratification" and "Seed Testing" in chapter 7, "The Terrarium as Nursery.")

Another rewarding aspect of glass gardening happens to be a specialty of my own, and I shall devote an entire chapter to it. Dried autumn arrangements acquire a new look in covered glass containers, and these bottled bouquets will last indefinitely. (See chapter 8, "Dried Arrangements Under Glass.") The possibilities are limited only by your own ingenuity; you need neither training nor skill with brush or paints to create attractive designs from dried fern fronds, flowers and grasses, pressed under the glass of a picture frame. Fern fronds, with a little imagination, can be converted into Christmas trees for display over a mantel or into portable personal holiday greetings.

Finally, this is not a hobby for adults alone. Gardening in bottles has tremendous appeal for children. And for shut-ins, there is no more workable or satisfying way of bringing the outdoors inside,

A 3-foot high quintet of fish bowls on a tripod holds goldfish (soon to be moved to a large tank); green plant and variegated box; variegated wax plant, hoya, and a figurine; nephthytis, table fern and peperomia; and baby's tears. Coffee can plastic lids are the covers. Quintet bauble by Morgantown Glass Guild; plantings by Nosegay-at-the-Carlyle.

offering as it does intriguing and absorbing work for the hands, and the possibility of watching the wondrous functionings of nature without leaving one's own room.

THE TERRARIUM AND I

I became interested in glass gardening when I was a boy. I paid frequent and extended visits to a favorite aunt who lived in an old colonial farmhouse, and one of the delights of this rural habitat were her window sills in winter. Such a luxuriant array of plants could grow only where cows were kept. But the focal points of her displays were the many small bowls and jars filled with partridge-berry and moss. An image from my childhood that time cannot erase is my aunt's glass hen, sitting on a nestful of brilliantly colored berries. The Connecticut snows were often a foot deep, but the resplendent growths and glories of summertime were preserved throughout the year in these miniature worlds of berried greenery; it was, I'm sure, those jars of bright berries that attracted me, for keeps, to the fascinating hobby of growing plants in glass.

I was *not* successful from the word go. Either I forgot the drainage gravel and charcoal, or overwatered, or I expected the impossible of the wrong plants. But I learned rapidly from my mistakes, improved through trial and error, and was soon able to share my successful experiments with other potential enthusiasts through a series of magazine articles. It was the reader response to these bottle-garden magazine feature stories that gave birth to this book.

It's not my purpose to write a technical manual. I won't use terminology that sends you running to an encyclopedia. My aim is to tell you how to create, plant and care for glass gardens with a minimum expenditure of time and effort. I write as a veteran bottle-stuffer, with dirt under his fingernails and a fund of first-hand, home-grown experience. May you profit from my mistakes; it's very difficult to tell someone how to do something you've done instinctively—have you ever tried to pin down a natural-born, instinctive cook to a firm, step-by-step recipe? I think you'll have no trouble following the pragmatic planting procedures I've outlined here, but I hope that once you get your glass garden bearings, you'll also venture forth on your own. Experience, mistakes included, remains the most reliable of all instructors.

THE TERRARIUM AND YOU

I'll use the term "glass gardens" to cover bottles, crystal gardens, berry bowls, candy jars, ferneries, plantariums, terrariums and Wardian cases (see Chapter 1). Derived from the Latin *terra* (earth), the word terrarium is further defined as a bottle, bowl, or other container enclosing a garden of plants—or housing small animals. As you become a glass garden enthusiast, you'll find yourself appraising every transparent container as a prospective garden setting. And, as a corollary, you'll be on the perpetual lookout for that certain plant, pebble or figurine to set off a given bottled landscape you've got in mind.

Just as the process of moisture condensing inside a corked bottle is a never-ceasing cycle, so gardening in glass containers is an adventure without end. Whether you use it as a hobby, as a profitable avocation, or as a practical means of growing wanted or needed plant life, where your glass garden is, that's where the action is too. There are containers and plants to find; tanks to landscape; bowls, jugs and jars to plant, and endless bottles to conquer.

Our case rests—our case, that is, of glass. People in glass houses are advised not to throw stones, but people who cultivate glass gardens —and may you soon become one of them—are among the eternally fortunate; they have left boredom and sterility behind them, and are too busy arranging their pebbles to think of throwing them.

And now let's start at the very beginning.

1.

THE ORIGINS OF

GLASS GARDENS

THE GARDENS OF ADONIS

Our pagan precursors were well acquainted with the principles of gardening inside of a container, and with the capacity of such artificial surroundings to force vegetation into premature bloom.

The legend, both Greek and Phoenician (the latter being a link with even more ancient Semitic cultures) is that Adonis, the beloved slain amour of the goddess of love known to the Phoenicians as Astarte and to the Greeks as Aphrodite, was resurrected annually in the festival called the Adonia, during which the celebrants first lamented his death and then rejoiced over his resurrection. This myth is commonly regarded as symbolic of the cyclic decay and regeneration of all vegetation, represented concretely, at these annual festivals, by the *Gardens of Adonis,* our first known instance of forced plant growth in sealed containers. These "gardens" were, in actuality, baskets or pots, probably of earthenware, in which quick-growing plants were sealed for an eight-day period. They were first tended, then allowed to wither, and ultimately tossed into the sea, together with an image of the dead Adonis. Death, life; again death. Plato's *Phaedon* confirms that if a grain of seed or the branch of a tree were placed in these "gardens," it would indeed mature in eight days.

THE SURGEON AND THE BOTTLE: THE STRANGE CASE OF DR. NATHANIEL WARD

So the Greeks, as usual, knew the answers, but also as usual, this answer lay dormant during era upon era. The fact is that glass gardening, as we know it today, did not begin until the early decades of the 19th century. In the summer of 1829, a certain Dr. Nathaniel Bagshaw Ward, surgeon by profession, natural historian by avocation, observed that in the moist soil contained in a sealed bottle where he had buried the chrysalis of a sphinx moth, a fern and some grass had sprouted!

Dr. Ward was understandably intrigued. He identified the vegetation as *Poa annua* and *Lastreae felixmas*. He watched the bottled proceedings vigilantly. And lo, the grass flowered and the ferns produced new fronds annually until, after some four years, the entire verdant miracle went haywire because the lid had rusted and no longer provided the needed sealing. The vegetation died, but not before it had served its instructive purpose.

Why, wondered Dr. Ward, couldn't plants be transported in airtight containers, flourishing en route just as they had in his sooty waterfront garden? Accordingly, in 1832, he filled two glass cases with ferns and grasses, and packed them off to Sydney, Australia, in those days eight months distant by sea. When the plants arrived, they were thriving, even though no water whatsoever had been added to the cases lashed to the deck. The globe-trotting greenhouses had weathered extreme changes of temperature, ranging from freezing cold to intense heat, and were none the worse for weather or wear.

Dr. Ward's Australian colleagues promptly refilled the cases, and sent them around the Cape of Good Hope, with equal success. Ward, convinced, published his findings in 1842 in an article entitled "On the Growth of Plants in Closely Glazed Cases." The excited terrarium pioneer wrote, "We may without any stretch of imagination carry our minds back to the primeval condition of vegetation when the Lord God had not caused it to rain upon the earth, and there was not a man to till the ground. But there went up a mist upon the earth and watered the whole face of the ground." This condition he likened to the independent state of plants in sealed glass.

GLASS AND GLOBAL HORTICULTURE

By mid-century, Wardian Cases, as the portable greenhouses had come to be known, were traveling the seven seas. In this way, some 20,000 tea plants were shipped from Shanghai to the Himalayas, giving birth to the entire Indian tea industry—and this when all previous attempts at shipping such plants had failed. Wardian Cases also accounted for the introduction of Chinese bananas into Fiji and Samoa, and of Brazilian rubber trees into Ceylon. Quinine, a product of the South American Chinchona tree, came to British India via a Wardian Case.

And, of course, non-commercial horticulture profited immensely from the new shipping method. Common garden plants from both Europe and America underwent continental interchange via Wardian Cases; one London nursery utilized 500 of them within a seven-year period, and it's said that Kew, the Royal Botanical Garden, imported more plants in a scant fifteen years than in the entire preceding century! The quest for plants became global rather than regional, and the greenhouse industry boomed.

The U.S.A. got in the act, as usual. In 1857, our Congress contracted to procure Chinese tea plants with the hope of establishing a native tea industry. In terms of transport, the experiment was a rousing success: many of the 35,000 plants had germinated right in the cases prior to their arrival in Washington. But the experiment as a whole was a fizzle: tea-growing didn't work out in our Southern states, largely because of the Civil War and the resultant lack of available slave labor—which is why nearly all of our teas still come from China and India.

Dr. Ward, as is the case with many a man whose experiments have altered history's byroads if not the main routes, died relatively obscure and in no wise wealthy. He remained the inquisitive discoverer of a fern and some blades of grass in a sealed jar. But we, forever in his debt, have gardens in glass.

2.

CONTAINERS, PLAIN

AND FANCY

In the terrain of the terrarium, there need never be such a thing as the wrong setting for your interior furnishings or vice versa. Yours is the privilege of appropriate selection. You can pick the glass house for your chosen plants from every conceivable kind of container. You'll want a terrarium that's proportioned and related to your home setting; then you can exercise a free hand as to its landscaping, and as to the plants and accessories that will inhabit it.

I'm devoting this chapter to a survey of the many categories of terrariums available—those for aesthetic glass gardening, and also the functional glass or plastic coverings you may want to use for the practical purposes described below.

You start, you understand, with a wide-open door. In theory, at least. Almost any clear glass container that you can plug, cork or cover has the basic makings of an attractive garden setting. I said, *clear* glass; light-colored amber or green-tinted glass—and so many intriguing containers are made of one or the other—will indeed admit sufficient light for plant growth. But unless your mind's-eye plan is a plant silhouette that stresses pure outline and not color, use only clear, untinted glass.

As to size, depending on the current level of your manual dexterity and the space available, your selection can run the gamut, from the diminutive pill bottle to the spacious dimensions of a plantarium.

Collecting containers is half the fun. Once you get underway, you'll see every and anything made out of glass (or plastic) in terms of its planting potential. My own friends, often the recipients of handsome garden-in-glass gifts as a reward for the bread they've cast on the waters, have been more than generous in bequeathing me their leaky aquariums and emptied gift decanters. Whenever the clutter becomes overwhelming and I decide to discard some earlier-treasured container, I find that during the intervening years it's become a collector's item. I'm no good at getting rid of terrariums.

Let me prod your imagination with a listing of some of the more likely categories.

THE TANK TERRARIUM OR OBLONG PLANTER

This is the glass garden classic. Tank-type terrariums, in addition to giving you maximum gardening and landscaping freedom, possess some of the decorative versatility of hi-fi units and contemporary cabinets: they can be placed on shelves—in wall niches, closets, or on display bookcases, where they're illuminated by artificial light. Used in this way, they make highly effective accessories for room-dividers.

The aquarium, of course, is the traditional tank container. These square glass cases are available in several, even multiple gallon, sizes, and you can find them wherever pet supplies of any scope are sold. Old tanks no longer suitable for fish turn up in second-hand stores, in auctions, and at the always-popular tag-sale. In the course of the years, I've acquired an entire shelfful. The newer aquariums are bound in stainless steel, but non-stainless banding can be painted to match the decor of your room.

The actual glass garden case, or terrarium proper, is currently being manufactured in plastic and fiber glass cases. Aside from plastic's greatest drawback, its scratchability, they're just as attractive as their glass predecessor, and as they're non-corrosive, they don't require repainting. Some models offered by terrarium suppliers come with plastic covers that fit securely over an enameled watertight base.

MAKING YOUR OWN CONTAINER

You needn't buy, of course; you can make your own, using a glass and cement sealant purchasable at any sizeable housewares store, masking tape, and pieces of ordinary window glass.

To make a 5½-gallon terrarium, cut the following pieces of glass:

Two 8" x 10" pieces for the end walls

Two 16" x 10" pieces for the sides

Two 16" x 8¼" pieces for the cover and base.

Larger or smaller planters may be scaled to your dimensions.

Clean and dry each piece of glass thoroughly. Then, cut 12 strips of masking tape in 3-inch lengths. Join the 4 wall pieces and tape them firmly. Next, tape the walls to the bottom glass; take care not to leave any gaps. Then apply the sealant to the *inside* seams. Any necessary tooling must be done immediately, before the sealant hardens. After the sealant has dried thoroughly, trim it with a razor blade, but cut carefully so as not to undercut the sealant. Any misplaced sealant should be wiped off the glass at once with a dry cloth. Allow the sealant to set for a day or two before you do any planting. Tape all sharp edges, or else buff them before assembling, so as to prevent nicked wrists and knuckles.

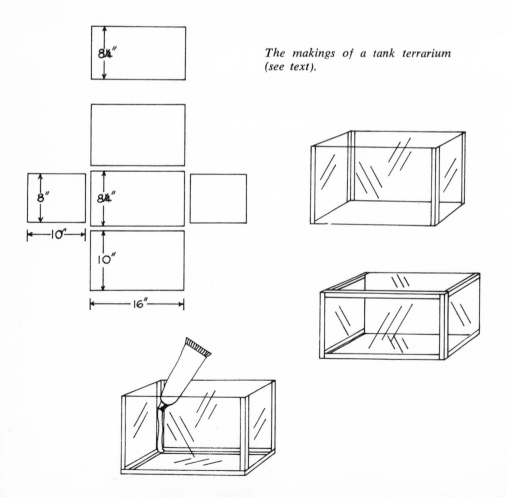

The makings of a tank terrarium (see text).

A stainless steel-and-plate-glass tank terrarium with a removable glass top is planted with bright-fruited partridgeberry (foreground) accenting a central feature of variegated rattlesnake plantain and spotted wintergreen. At either end are princess pine, pipsissewa and shining club moss; treelike 8-inch club moss gives background height.

PLANTARIUMS

These spacious, handsome containers (see Sources of Supply) are the ideal vehicles for displaying potted plants. They come in 3-foot and 4-foot lengths, and are 19½ inches wide and 22 inches high. The well-designed case is framed in aluminum, and is mounted on tapered hardwood legs, so that the plant display actually sits at a height of 46 inches. Trays of sand and pebbles, on which pots are set, provide constant moisture. Plantariums duplicate weather conditions suited to various plant needs: either temperate warmth or tropical humidity is created by the adjustment of the sliding front glass panels. Temperature and moisture content are read by a thermometer and hygrometer. And the terrarium's not dependent on your available daylight supply—or lack of it: it's equipped with fixtures that can provide either Gro-lux or white fluorescent artificial light. (See chapter 5, "An ABC of Glass Garden Maintenance; Artificial Light and Windowless Glass Gardening.")

21

BOWLS, BRANDY SNIFTERS, BOTTLES AND BAUBLES: NON-OBLONG CONTAINERS IN EVERY SHAPE AND FORM

FISH BOWLS

These are the rounded, flatsided bowls, and they are an old standby. You can get them in many different sizes, and they are as practical as they are inexpensive. Their only drawback is that the glass is frequently of an inferior quality.

Any clear container with a pencil-plus-sized opening will do. Here are a glass teapot, a plastic Easter egg, a covered salt dish, a liquor bottle, an old medicine bottle, a Mason jar, a nursing bottle and a wine bottle, all waiting to house gardens.

BRANDY SNIFTERS

The oversized brandy glass is an ideal container. These always-glamorous stemmed planters are easy to plant and to cover; they appeal both to period and contemporary tastes, and the quality of glass may be very good indeed. The half-gallon size is a favorite with inebriates and florists alike, but gallon glasses give you more scope for creativeness and for plant expansion. The smaller and more malleable snifters make attractive berry bowls. The brandy snifter is a natural for the plant hobbyist keen on displaying a prize bloom, and makes a superb blossom bowl.

BOTTLE PLANTERS

With these, the field is wide open. Bottle gardens can be grown in almost any transparent container. Remember, however, that you're the one doing the planting, and the only way to get a plant inside a bottle is to *put* it there. Acquire only those whose openings you can see your planting way into. Generally I consider any bottle with an opening the size of a dime as fair game. Anything smaller must be approached with caution, but depending on the skill and patience you can command, it needn't be ruled out.

We've already mentioned gift decanters, but ordinary everyday wine and liquor bottles offer unlimited opportunities for interior plant decoration. (Unlimited except for the size of the opening!)

Miniatures

Provided that they fall within the acceptable color categories, the little bottles that contained iodine, tinctures and olive oil shouldn't be overlooked, nor should the plastic medicinal containers of our aspirin age. (Plastic is as usable as glass.) Perfume bottles, mentioned above, have smaller openings, but their unusual and distinctive shapes make them very showy planters. Apothecary jars are another rich source of supply for miniature containers.

Old Medicine Bottles

Many of these are hand-blown, and their most appealing idiosyncrasies may be their pitfalls: inspect them carefully for irregularities in the thickness of the glass, swellings, lumps, and false bottoms.

A half-gallon cider jug with an opening 1" in diameter contains a 7" palm. Living sphagnum holds soil tapped through a funnel. Gravel and pebbles are the ground covers.

These miscalculations on the part of the glass-blower (or shrewd and deceptive calculation by the less ethical purveyor of the old style home remedy cure-all) can cause planting problems if they elude your attention.

Cider Jugs Used as Display Domes

Half-gallon and gallon-size cider jugs are both attractive and easy to plant. Moreover, they can be used to make display domes. Proceed as follows: fasten a band of flat wire around the upper half of the jug, and tighten it with pliers. Remove the wire (slipping it off, thus tightly coiled), and heat it until the metal glows. Then, using pliers, drop the wire back around the jug, which you now submerge in a pail of cold water. If the wire is both tight and hot enough, the jug should break neatly in half. If at first you don't succeed, try, etc. Now put on some gloves, and smooth the rough edges with sandpaper. The lower portion of the jug becomes a handsome display dome. But don't discard the upper half with its handle. You can cork it, and use it for covering individual plants.

ANTIQUE GLASS

Nothing more beautiful than old glass, but lay off expensive bottles until you've achieved a modicum of skill at planting through narrow-necked openings. Occasionally, you'll be fortunate enough to track down an ornate wooden-framed Victorian fern case. Antique shops, both town and country, offer a tempting array of apothecary and spice jars, stoppered decanters, glass teapots, candy and tobacco jars, as well as random stemmed goblets and covered dishes. Anything goes. Cracker and cookie jars from the Country Store make commodious planters, as do the five-quart glass butter churns from a less hectic era.

JARS AND HOUSEHOLD MISCELLANY

This all-embracing category can be considered the proletariat of glass-garden containers. It includes most of the glass containers found on supermarket and pharmacy shelves that are used for packaging jelly, baby foods, condiments, pickles, perfume, detergents, medicine and lotion. Actually there is nothing particularly proletarian about a shapely perfume bottle; it can be turned into a fertile aristocrat of a container. Incidentally, asparagus spears are packed upside down in glasses that can be inverted over plants and dried displays. (Glass containers work both ways!)

CLOCHES AND KEEPSAKE DOMES

We mentioned these in the opening sentence of the Foreword. They

Some 2 inches of growing medium is spread over the base (a painted clay saucer). Then comes an 8" aluminum plant, a 7" variegated corn and a peperomia, a 5" maranta, and, in the foreground, crinkle-leafed peperomia and strawberry begonia. The cat has its own gravel patch. After plants are lightly sprinkled, the dome is inverted over the base.

are used for displaying everlastings and bonsai landscapes (see chapter 3). Depending upon whether they're made of true 19th century glass or are plastic imitations, they come in different sizes and prices. The plastic variety can certainly serve your purpose, but remember that plastic scratches easily; if you can find the real thing, so much the better. Buy it. Or inherit it.

MISCELLANEOUS GLASS CONTAINERS

Let your own fancy roam free. Seize upon a rose or bubble bowl, a candy jar, a pear-shaped container. Toilet soap often comes in intriguing glass containers. As do bath salts. Old coffee makers (and some new ones, too) and water pitchers may offer the makings of just the house your plants are looking for.

HANGING PLANTERS

We move to a somewhat different category. Not all glass gardens need sit. They can hang. Any lightweight container with a neck that can be securely suspended from wire is suitable for a hanging garden. Some glass manufacturers, in fact, have played right into your hands by blowing special planters with side openings for convenient planting. Prices vary according to quality, size, and craftsmanship.

Laboratory Flasks

Who can resist them? Not I. These round-bottomed bottles, sturdy yet light, can be procured from pharmaceutical suppliers, and their simple lines render them splendid accessories. Suspend them on strong but extremely fine picture wire.

NOVELTY PLANTERS

If I begin to sound a little wild at this point, bear with me. Once you start planting, you'll perceive the possibilites of what seem to be highly unlikely objects. Besides Christmas tree ornaments and Easter eggs of glass and plastic, there are candy-filled Valentine heart-shaped boxes, not to mention animals and, in season, Santa Clauses. Inventive plantings can be housed in glass fishing floats, nursing bottles, children's plastic play blocks, and in maple-syrup bottle-banks shaped like bears, other animals and even people. If these seem to far-fetched, just move on.

Three bottlefuls of plants: (from left) miniature ivy with plenty of room to sprawl in the violin bottle; a prayer plant growing in ¾" of soil in a tapered decanter; partridgeberry cuttings rooted in moss and soil in a plastic heart.

Dr. Ward never dreamed of terrariums like this, but I couldn't resist a three-piece acrylic bubble food-server made by Raymor. It holds baby's tears and white aquarium gravel.

THE FUNCTIONAL TERRARIUM

MINIATURE GREENHOUSES

You can acquire numerous kinds of greenhouses for seed starting, rooting cuttings, and for plant display as well (see chapter 7, "The Terrarium as Nursery"). Get your seedlings off to an early start, and use the premises to show off your proud plantings as well. These greenhouses function at room temperature in natural light, or by artificial illumination and heating cables. Some models come with trays that are equipped with adjustable dividers; others have moveable ventilators in the lid. (See Sources of Supply.)

Crystalite Indoor Greenhouse

This deluxe miniature greenhouse (see Sources of Supply) measures 2 feet long, 2 feet high, and 18 inches wide; it will hold half a dozen 5-inch pots or four 6-inch pots. Quite a thing for the indoor plant-potter. The features are as follows: A heavy bottom plastic tray is held securely by sturdy legs that also support the vinyl-covered frame. Two fluorescent lamps fitted into the crown of the house burn 15-watt tubes. Brackets on the ends of each lamp secure the lights to the frame. Extra accessories include: a daily repeat timer that turns the lamps on and off at predetermined times so as to supply uniform, controlled lighting conditions; an automatic water feature, attached as an additional plastic tray underneath the unit, which feeds and waters plants in the "main floor" tray above through a fiber glass wick that functions by capillary action. . . . What will they think of next?

Although this greenhouse is primarily designed for potted plants, it may also be planted as a terrarium.

CONTAINERS FOR OUTDOOR PLANT PROTECTION

Like indoor plants, field-grown seedlings and transplants (see chapter 7) benefit from the protection of various covering devices. In addition to plastic bags, there are the following:

In-the-Row Plastic Greenhouse (see Sources of Supply)

A recent innovation, this greenhouse is available in 5-foot lengths. It measures 12 inches high by 12 inches wide; several lengths will shelter an entire row of tender annuals. It admits sun and warmth, yet shuts out rain, wind, and cold.

Small shelters

The versatile plastic-lidded coffee can does double terrarium duty. With its bottom left on, it's a kind of little terrarium with a skylight. But you can remove its tin bottom, and place it over a transplant; it'll receive sufficient light through the plastic cover. It's a handy and economic means of retaining moisture and affording weather protection for newly set-out seedlings.

Then there's the aptly-named and convenient Hotkap (see Sources of Supply), which has been on the market for years. This weather-resistant, waxed paper-like dome provides protection against frost and wind for individual plants, and wards off insects as well.

THE ABSENTEE GARDENER: TERRARIUMS FOR THE TURNED BACK

Off for July? Or for February, the new trend? Let the glass garden be your potted plant guardian in either case. For vacation storage, use the clay pots with bottom drainage holes. Put any that'll fit in unused terrariums whose bottoms are well spread with gravel. Cover the tank or tanks securely with tightly fitted glass or plastic. As for those plants too large for glass, pot them as well, and slip them into moisture-tight bags of polyethylene plastic (holeless!) that are tied tightly around the lower stems. Now trot off to ski or surf or climb an Alp.

THE VOYAGING COLLECTOR: TERRARIUMS FOR TRAVELING

Seeds, cuttings, plants and seedlings are the inevitable trophies of the plant collector (always with the local conservation rules firmly in mind, as well as those governing illegal interstate transportation of plant material). I keep a moss-filled tank terrarium in the car trunk for larger specimens, tightly covered with plastic. On longer journeys, I open the trunk during stopovers to admit light. And of course, one can always remove plants from the trunk overnight. I've successfully transported conifer seedlings during midsummer heat by backing the terrarium against the icechest. Sometimes, I've even dropped ice cubes into the terrarium, or placed plants in the icechest itself (always in plastic bags or containers).

Smaller plants and root balls of evergreens and other trophies travel nicely in plastic bags; plastic-lidded coffee tins, sandwich bags and aspirin bottles make good totes for seeds, as do moisture-tight bread and potato chip bags.

Closet shops and hardware stores abound in plastic utility boxes designed for storing hats, shoes and small tools. These all make fine nurseries, and excellent lightweight traveling cases for vacationing plant collectors. Other plastic naturals are cake and bread boxes, individual containers for sandwiches and wedges of pie, and numerous smaller boxes used for packaging and displaying merchandise.

Plastic soap boxes and, yes, toothbrush holders can accommodate one or several seedlings in moist moss, and fit nicely in your pocketbook or suitcase.

BOTTLED AND SEALED: COVER WITH CARE

Whether you are covering a living garden and wish to retain moisture, or keeping everlastings dry and dust-free, the cover you select or make *should be transparent,* unless the container is to be displayed on a shelf where no one will be peering into it from above. The considerations, of course, are both biologic and aesthetic: the living garden benefits from the additional light, and terrarium displays should be visible from all possible angles. Clearly this stipulation doesn't apply to bottle stoppers, whose size is fragmentary.

GLASS

If your terrarium is square, cover it with sheets of window or picture glass. If it's circular, there are numerous possibilities depending on size. Glass plates, available in almost any diameter required, make fine covers (and, by the way, bottoms too.) For smaller containers, consider watch crystals and dial faces from old clocks. If you cut your own glass, make certain that there are no jagged or overlapping edges. Follow the instructions given under "Making Your Own Terrarium," smoothing rough edges with sandpaper or covering them with tape. Glass cutting, of course, may not be your dish of tea, and it couldn't matter less: your local glass cutter will do the job for less than a dollar.

Square surfaces should be measured with meticulous care. For circular containers, either measure the diameter (with equal care), or take a tracing: invert the container, and outline the rim with a pencil. Then you'll know exactly what you need.

PLASTIC

Earlier in this chapter, I mentioned plastic coffee-can lids as excellent terrarium tops. You can also cut lids of all shapes from stiff plastic. But be warned that this lightweight material will require considerable taping so as to fit snugly. Temporary covers for nursery terrariums—those in which you're developing bulbs or seedlings for later transplant, can easily be concocted by stretching cellophane wrap, saran wrap or a similar product over the top, and securing it with tape, wire, or if your container is cylindrical, with elastic bands.

BOTTLE CORKS

If the bottle that's housing your glass garden is already equipped with a stopper, well and good. If not, use corks. They are attractive and tight-fitting, and can be bought in packages of assorted sizes. If your particular bottle seems to elude any standard size, take a sharp knife and gently whittle. The cork to a Thermos bottle (if you're willing to sacrifice your Thermos for the Cause) will often prove an ideal solution to the problem of fitting a large water bottle.

Always keep a supply of assorted corks on hand, but if you find yourself with a newly-created bottle garden and no suitable cork, seal it temporarily with cellophane tape.

3.

SHAPING A GARDEN IN GLASS:

Design and Landscape

An empty terrarium is a crystal ball, pregnant with possibilities: gaze into it, and see a verdant future entirely of your own making, a minia-ture world of your own creation. Your inner vision may conjure up a tropical landscape replete with lush, jungle-like vegetation. It could be the replica of a natural woodland glen—the renewal, perhaps, of a memory, or the concrete evocation of a deep-breathed dream. Perhaps, weary of the chaotic and unplanned ugliness that permeates so much of urban and suburban environmental life, you may elect to design a formal garden setting, tranquil, ordered, and elegant. You've a freedom of choice that could never be yours in whatever portion of the out-of-doors that fortune may have allotted you; in the world of the glass garden, you are architect, prime mover, king.

PLANS: MADE TO BE BROKEN

Whatever your predilection, certain inherent principles will obtain. And even as I remind you of some of them I'll proceed to contradict them here and there, because principle must bow to the exigencies of "what gives"; the realities and imponderables of what happens when you tangle with living matter, which always has ideas of its own. So plan to temper harmony with dissonance, rigidity with elasticity, and all of that. There's always, as someone who was not Confucius said, more than one way to skin a cat.

Nonetheless, here we go, modifying every inch of the way. You're dealing with a group of elements: moss, soil, rocks, plants and ac-

32

I. LEFT: *A holiday breakfast tray is decorated with a two-piece crystal egg holding dried foxtail, quaking grass, berried jewels-of-Opar, royal fern, a tiny acorn cup nest, tree ornaments, eggs and a bird— all glued into the bottom half of the egg. The rose would stay fresh for most of the holiday season in a glass egg (which is available in varied sizes).*

II. RIGHT: *A two-quart bubble bowl with a moss liner holds bloodleaf begonia, coleus, variegated rattlesnake plantain (central feature) and partridgeberry (foreground). Landscaping details: rocks and a pebbly beach.*

III. LEFT: *The planted brandy snifter shown in Plate IX is here the centerpiece for a luncheon table, but the duckling, too rustic for such use, has been removed.*

IV. LEFT: *Strawflowers, rose haws, grasses and royal fern fronds in candle lamps ornament a piano. The arrangement is scaled to size first, then the materials are wired together (be sure wire doesn't show) and inserted into tiny pinholder fastened to base with floral clay. The cover is added, and strips of dried moss dropped in to conceal the mechanics.*

V. BELOW: *The terrarium trio includes wax begonia, African violet 'Liberty Belle', wood fern and bright partridgeberry, raised under fluorescent lights but moved here for decoration. The pressed flower picture (see page 121 for technique), now several years old, is laid on a mat wound with red embroidery wool.*

cessories seasoned to taste; all of them must be related within the framework of a unified, harmonious presentation. (Even planned chaos can be harmonious.) So make a plan, but don't be afraid to revise it: you may be thwarted by an unruly root, and be forced to resort to an alternate choice. For myself, despite well-planned intentions, I frequently find it necessary to scrap the original planting. Improvisation, provided it's grounded in a real theme, may work out very well indeed.

PRINCIPLES, PLACEMENT, PROPORTION

So, first, harmony; second, simplicity. Don't overcrowd the scene. Even a highly intricate arrangement demands restraint, and by contrast a tuft of grass and a few beach pebbles may create a more striking effect than a very busy garden. Some of the most spectacular landscapes in all of nature, need I remind you, are sere, stark, and the more striking therefore.

Next, scaling and compatibility, the latter subject discussed under plant types and soil requirements. A single terrarium has got to be relatively homogeneous, in terms of plants with compatible soil, light and temperature predilections. As to scale: to dwell on this subject would be an insult to your intelligence. Try a dry run inside the terrarium, if you're using a tank or other open-orificed container; if not, do what you can on a tabletop. See how your plants conform to your garden picture. One may need its foliage trimmed, and the root ball of another may require reducing in order to fit into a narrow crevice.

Because, in a terrarium garden, you're really able to create an entire scene and not just a fragment, you may find it worth your while to work from all or part of an appealing photograph. This can be particularly helpful in guiding you as to scale. You may even measure individual elements, such as the height of a tree vis-à-vis a neighboring shrub or figure, and then transfer the proportions to your own creation. In fact, studying photographs of landscapes is an excellent way of developing your own inner view of what a variety of gardens in glass might look like. Look at paintings, too.

Don't think of your terrarium garden as a static proposition: the purpose of a garden is to grow, and this is another reason to avoid overcrowding, even if open spaces tempt you. Fill such gaps with moss and stones, pending the natural, inevitable extension of your plants.

Beware of group plantings that are so arranged, or non-arranged, that you can't tell the trees for the forest, and where all plant individuality gets swallowed up in an undifferentiated mass of lots of nothing. Exploit the individual characteristics of each plant by placing it where its form, coloring and plastic quality will be viewed most advantageously. Use pebble patches and rocky backgrounds for just this purpose.

PLANTING VIS-A-VIS LANDSCAPING

This may be the place to distinguish between planting and landscaping. In the former, plants predominate; in the latter, the contour and characteristics of the land are the feature attractions, and the planting evolves around them. You can devise an interesting landscape simply by sloping the soil upward, giving the effect of a hillside. Similarly, you can create a pair of hills, one in each rear corner, and span the valley between them by a bridge over a rocky stream. Or again, you may decide to slope the entire terrain to one side.

Mounded soil is retained with Featherock (see section on "The Rocky Look") or with a semicircle of tightly fitted stones. Using pieces of slate recessed with alternate layers of soil you can create crevices for planting tiny ferns and creeping things.

Remember that ambitious landscaping must be confined to tank terrariums and the larger-mouthed jugs. If you're working inside the confines of a bottle, you're stringently limited in your use of rocks, figurines and other ornaments, except for pebbles. True, you can build up shallow slopes with your dowel, then naturalize them with small stones—but you'll achieve your most valid and effective contrasts by the use of plants—taller ones inserted in the center of your bottle, flanked by growth of contrasting heights.

GROUNDWORK: REAR TO FORE AND VICE VERSA

Now for another general rule, an exception to which (the case of the upright bottle) we've just noted: *Start first with the taller background material,* planted in the rear. Then work your way forward, next filling in the central focal area, the foreground, and the sides until the landscape is complete. *Amendment,* right here and now: sometimes a landscaped rock garden is easier to plant if you start from center. Also, the tall-plants-to-the-rear formula is reversed in certain style landscapes: English gardens, for example, grade up. In such cases, your smallest plants can crown the background elevations, and the taller ones will look proportionately appropriate up front.

In the previous paragraph I spoke of *the central focal area.* The focal planting is a centrally located plant with sufficient visual power to tie the garden together. Its saliency may lie, not in its flamboyance, but in its simplicity. Foliage, for example, can be as spectacular as a flowering plant, which is not to decry the brilliant possibilities of the latter; African violets, wax begonias and partridgeberry patches make fine focal plantings.

Here are two lists to keep in mind when you plant for terrarium drama. In line with what I've just said, you may want to go spectacular with foliage, and the first list provides you with your plant ammunition. As for the florals (list 2), remember that a great many so-called foliage plants do produce, as a kind of bonus, flowers as well. But these are the really spectacular bloomers, the kind you'll want for sheer floral impact. See "Terrariums in Bloom" for more information on several of them.

The "tall" central plant in this 10-inch glass pear is an 8-inch Syngonium, serving as background for an inch plant and a bright-leaved coleus. In the center is a rattlesnake plantain; clearly visible in the foreground is a conifer seedling. All this plant life is supported by about 2½ inches of growing medium, cupped in an attractive liner of living sheet moss.

Plants with Brilliant or Variegated Foliage

aluminum plant
Bertolonia
bloodleaf
British soldier (*Cladonia*)
caladium
coleus
corn plant
croton
dumb cane (Dieffenbachia)
glacier ivy
grape fern
green plant

inch plant
ivy arum
pachysandra
prayer plant
rattlesnake fern
rattlesnake plantain
seersucker plant
snake plant
spotted pipsissewa
strawberry begonia
velvet plant
Zebrina

Flowering Plants

African violet
begonia
crocus sieberi
dwarf water lily
early saxifrage
foam flower
Jack-in-the-pulpit
lily-of-the-valley
liverleaf (*Hepatica*)

miniature gloxinia
periwinkle
Solomon's seal
spathe flower
viola
violet

Foreground planting serves as an invitation; its primary function is to lead the eye onward to further exploration. Like a low border in a flower bed, it should be harmonious with what lies beyond, and although appealing, not distracting. Suitable candidates for this location are low, sprawling plants such as berryless partridge vines and kenilworth ivy, flat stones or pebbly beaches, and patches of moss or lichens. Reserve your smallest plants for this area. You can use small-sized, larger-growing specimens, but do so only where replacement and transplantings offer no problem, because they'll grow to the point of obstructing the scene beyond, and you'll have to shift.

Here is a list of vine-like sprawlers, creepers and spacefillers, exclusive of mosses and lichens. Don't get the idea that all of these just hug the soil; many of them are fairly tall. But each of them is

A candy jar planter offers fine viewing of an arrangement bedded in moss nestling deep in its base. The focal features are rattlesnake plantain and spotted wintergreen; partridgeberry sprawls gracefully and brightly about the sides, and club mosses (shining, tree) comprise the background. (Photo courtesy Grillet's Nature Novelties)

eminently serviceable as a foreground planting or for giving a fuller, more lush look to your glass garden. Some of these creepers grow berries; others have blooms to offer now and again; check the Plant Encyclopedia for details.

Creeping Plants for Fillers and Foreground Planting

baby's tears (*Helxine*)	potato vine
bugleweed (*Ajuga*)	running myrtle (periwinkle)
creeping loosestrife	*Sedum acre*
grape ivy	Selaginella
inch plant	snowberry
ivy	trailing arbutus
Kenilworth ivy	twinberry
partridgeberry	wild ginger
philodendron	Zebrina

Your plants placed, take time to reconnoiter. Have you maintained a consistent harmonious unity throughout, and is the garden properly proportioned? You've still got time for revisions before the plants take root in their new surroundings. Could the focal plant be dramatized by a rock formation? Does the foreground lack interest?

You don't need to complete the garden in a single planting. You may do better by spreading the process over several sessions, being selective, and placing just the right plant in the right place as you acquire it. Terrariums needn't be built in a day.

If you're confronted with a few gaps or unsightly bare patches, cover them with bits of moss pressed into the soil; wads of shredded sphagnum can be used as well.

ADDED ATTRACTIONS (OR, THE PLOT THICKENS)

LIVELY SPACE-FILLERS AND ACCENTS

Another source of space-filling growth are the quick-germinating seeds of moisture-loving plants. Sprinkle fine seed thinly over moist moss or pebbles; larger seed can be pushed out of sight while it's hatching. Grass seed provides instant action; if it's fresh, it'll germinate in a very few days, and luxuriant little green lawn patches can be a glass garden delight. Remember that rapid-growing grass needs to be trimmed, so confine your use of it to garden areas that are readily accessible and easy to maintain. Another growing accessory suggestion is *white clover,* which, however, tends to produce long stems under glass, so locate it strategically. And sow the seed thinly so as to prevent molding. An *acorn,* dropped in after a brief stratification period, can add interest to a so-so foreground. Another multi-purpose and malleable space-filler is the *Jack-in-the-Pulpit,* my particular favorite. It starts out as oval leaflets, which are soon followed by miniature arum trifoliates. Then a tiny corm develops, and, while the plant is still small, it produces flowers! A wonderful little evolutionary parade in rapid tempo.

For accents, consider, first, temporary color spots provided by forsythia and other quick-flowering deciduous twigs (see chapter 6); of the permanent variety, try small stones suggesting natural outcroppings, or patches of white aquarium gravel, which can provide effective contrast to what may appear the green monotony of moss and foliage.

THE ROCKY LOOK: TAKE IT FOR GRANITE

Rocks give the miniature landscape an authentic look of the out-of-doors. You'll select your stones and pebbles for their appealing shape or color, their size and weight, and their all-over appropriateness to the scene you have in mind. Beaches, river bottoms, desert areas and mountain regions are all good rock hunting grounds. Often, you can find small flat stones for layering hillsides or paving garden paths at the foot of rocky cliffs blasted out by highway cut-throughs. Alternatively, you can break up clay or cinder blocks into realistic rock pieces. Coal, strikingly enough, can be attractive in certain settings. And, as we incessantly seem to wind up saying, if you can't find them or improvise them, you can always buy them. More convenient at times; much less fun.

Here in my own New England, I'm blessed with a backyard bordered with stone walls and rockpiles. Occasionally I happen upon coveted treasures such as pieces of Tufa, a lightweight porous limestone that often, when aged, becomes hoary with moss.

Featherock (see Sources of Supply)

On several occasions I've all but pulled my arms out of their sockets toting the heavy terrarium landscapes to editorial offices for photographs. Then, as the commercials say, Featherock entered my life, and everything's been different ever since: I now find that a landscaped garden in glass need be no heavier than the combined weight of soil and container.

First, to define it: Featherock is a native volcanic stone, quarried exclusively in the Sierra Nevadas. It comes in silver-grey and in charcoal. It is, as I say, volcanic, and was created from molten lava that cooled into fantastic shapes. Its porosity was caused by escaping gases. Although completely rugged in appearance, it's light enough to break with a hammer and chisel.

Now, here is the beauty part: you can use it in two highly effective ways: outside your tank, and in its interior.

For housing a tank terrarium in a natural setting, Featherock comes in slabs that measure up to 8 feet. Order a slab about 8 inches longer, 4 inches taller and 4 inches deeper than the container it's going to surround. Then, on the slab, outline the length and width of the terrarium with a chisel, leaving the 4-inch margin on top, at the rear, and on the three sides. (The word "slab" may be misleading; please think in three dimensions; perhaps "chunk" would be a better term.) Anyway, the front, or side from which the container is viewed, is of course open. Now hollow out the rock by sawing, chipping or chiseling, until the terrarium fits snugly, for a natural outdoor look, but can still be slipped easily in and out. Smooth the edges with a file, saving all of the better residual bits and pieces for other terrarium landscaping projects.

For interior use, you can buy it already in bits and pieces; its greatest asset is that it provides lightweight, natural-looking rocks inside the glass garden.

A chunk of rock makes a natural and effective base for this well-proportioned planting, in a stemmed candy jar, of rattlesnake plantain, partridgeberry and club mosses. The full height and width of the container are utilized, yet here is no crowding of materials, and each plant commands full visual attention.

An ingenious idea for a rocky, mountainous landscape is the use of a layer, perhaps ½ inch thick, of plaster of Paris, used as a holder for assorted rocks. After the plaster has dried, spaces between the rocks can be filled in with soil or sphagnum, and planted with whatever suits.

MINIATURE POOLS

What a strategically placed mirror can do for a home interior, the pool can do for your glass garden scene: terrarium landscapes can be reflected in anything that holds a few drops of water. Bottle caps, jar lids, ashtrays, coasters, soap dishes, pie plates, saucers, cups, bowls, salt dishes are all items suitable for conversion into garden ponds, preferably with irregular shorelines. Even quart-sized bowls capable of housing fish or turtles won't be out of place in a generous-sized terrarium landscape. I've used baking dishes as wide as a half-gallon brandy snifter for garden settings.

If you bury a round or square container in the soil and then rim it with moss and an occasional stone, you'll achieve the effect of a very realistic little pond. Sprinkle a few patches of grass on damp poolside moss, and you'll approximate the effect of sedges. Conceal a long narrow plastic box in moss, and you've got a brook. You can suggest the look of water with a mirror, or with gravel and an arching miniature bridge—but why? Water is easily come by, adds tremendous verisimilitude to the scene, and enhances the garden enormously by reflecting the plants around it.

For a special suggestion about pools for terrariums that are also vivariums, see the section on "Turtles" in chapter 11.

FIGURINES AND MINIATURE GARDEN ORNAMENTS (see Sources of Supply)

In this department of terrarium decor, both your imagination and acquisitive instincts can go hogwild. Small statuettes—human or animal or whatever—and miniature everythings can add the finishing touch (and "finishing" can mean both completing and ruining,

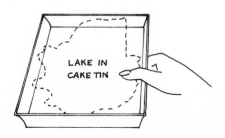

LAKE IN CAKE TIN

depending on how sensible you are) to your garden settings. Assemble a collection any way you like. Browse through antique, gift and florist shops. Dime stores and mail-order catalogues are fair game as well. Don't clutter up, or detract from an attractive gardenscape with inappropriate ornamentation. And money isn't the key: it can be costly and fancy and still be all wrong. If you have a ceramic leprechaun and a terrarium bowl of March shamrocks, clearly they are

An interesting arrangement with a shore-like feel features a clump of grass in a setting of beach pebbles, with a ceramic frog adding an aquatic touch. The cookie-jar container is 9 inches tall, and the pebbles are 2¼ inches deep. Although no moss liner has been used, a generous ball of earth ensures ample nourishment for the grass roots.

made for one another, but the same sprite could look ludicrous in another setting.

On the positive side, skilful and discreet use of figurines can do much for a garden in glass. A small animal can impart to short plants an effect of height, and so give the illusion of spaciousness to a small planting area. Figures create contrast, too; a colorful statuette can compensate for the lack of floral hues in a foliage bowl. An elephant or tiger (remember the toy counter as a source of supply) will intensify the mystery of a tropical jungle planting; a rabbit and turtle, properly matched as to size, could illustrate the hare-tortoise fable, etc. However, other animal-reptile combinations, lacking such a comfortable frame of reference, might be disturbing. Avoid religious figurines unless they are in good taste, appropriate to the planting theme, and conducive to reverence.

A happy aspect of terrarium sculpture, denied to outdoor garden sculpture because of its size, weight and cost, is that an assortment of miniature figurines is easily changed and/or moved about.

Other garden ornamentation includes bridges, benches, bird baths, bird houses, sun dials, gazing globes, gates, fences, etc., all, of course, scaled to terrarium size. Pieces of driftwood add great beauty and authenticity to a by-the-seascape. Realistic-looking ceramic toadstools and lichens can add authenticity and atmosphere to woodland plantings.

VISTAS UNDER GLASS

THE JAPANESE GARDEN

Meticulously wrought illusion is the basis of Japanese landscaping. Perspective is achieved by relationships. The placing of large-leafed plants in the foreground, fine-leaved ones at a distance, and middle-sized specimens somewhere in between can give a startlingly larger-than-life impression of infinite distance.

Accessories, scaled to the landscape, might include lanterns, bridges, Buddhas (lots of them around these days!), pagodas, etc. You can suggest boulders with stones, a log with a lichen-covered stick; a seedling conifer emerges as a perfectly proportioned tree. Sand, gravel and pebbles all have their place in the Japanese landscape.

Here again I suggest that you study a photograph or even a stylized drawing. Pick a scene that attracts you; measure it in terms of the height and width of the masses and solids. The keynote of all Japanese art, stylized gardens included, is the heaven-earth-man (vertical-horizontal-transitional, respectively) form.

Bonsai

A bonsai is a tree, shrub and occasionally a vine that has been grown in a small container, by dint of restrictive root, leaf and trunk pruning. The goal of the bonsai gardener is to create the look of a natural landscape of some antiquity. The terrain is characterized by ruggedness and austerity. This is *not* the natural look. Although any terrarium of generous proportions is technically suitable, the best con-

Plant a saikei landscape in a fish bowl. Use conifer seedlings (see list on page 46), a lake (in a cake tin), rocks, pebbles, and a miniature bridge.

tainers for a bonsai landscape are the gallon-sized brandy glasses or glass domes: they'll display the curious beauty of these compositions to their best advantage.

The best specimen for your bonsai tree is a seedling whose roots have already been confined in a pot, and whose trunk is relatively heavy in relation to the size of its branches and leaves. Black pine, juniper, spruce, cedar, and Japanese fruit trees are often used; a tree some 6 to 12 inches high should suit you best. The tree is planted in the traditional earth-colored bonsai container; rocks and wood are often added. (As I said above, the effect is deliberately a stark one.) When tiny models of bridges, figures, etc. are included, the result is termed *bonkei*.

It's best to buy your conifer in a can at the nursery (see Sources of Supply), because the roots will already have made their adjustment to confinement, but if you can dig your own specimen and prefer to do so, dig it right after a rain. Unearth it with as much soil as possible, wrap the roots in damp burlap, and plant it as quickly as possible. Rocky, deprived sites and cold climates produce seedlings with the greatest capacity for compromise; scout around for likely specimens in rocky, wooded areas. Sometimes seeds lodging in crevices develop contorted forms in their struggle to survive on minimal nutrients and moisture; they've already made their adjustment to life's vagaries, of which containers like terrariums and bonsai pots are but another example.

Saikei

Saikei embraces the aesthetic traditions of bonsai, but it allows greater freedom in composition. Comprising several varieties of plants, and allowing the use of traditional accessories, it's a perfect point of departure for the terrarium-grower. Use a roomy oblong planter, and include Featherock, aquarium gravel, and such plants as cedar, boxwood, ivy and clumps of grass. As to the trees: saikei uses the bonsai techniques for shaping, but it gives more emphasis to naturalness. A saikei tree looks as though the terrain and weather conditions of its terrain, rather than the grower, had determined its form. A saikei landscape can give you the feeling that this miniature vista differs only in size from the magnificence of nature's own composition. Try one.

Conifer and Deciduous Seedlings for Bonsai and Saikei Landscapes
(see Sources of Supply)

balsam fir

bristlecone pine

concolor (kon'kul-or) fir

Douglas fir

Fraser fir

Hondo spruce

Mugho pine

pin oak

Serbian spruce

Siberian pea tree

yew

OTHER GARDEN AND DESIGN NOTES

For a woodland garden, avoid sharp edges in paths; forms should be free. In a more formal setting, the balance will be static. Stateliness and dignity are suggested by strong vertical forms. If you want your glass-enclosed environment to exude quiet, serenity, and a degree of civilization, lay out a symmetrical pattern of tailored fence and and elegant pool. It's not Versailles, mind you, but it's quiet and orderly. For an old-fashioned design, use slips of such houseplant favorites as wax begonias, African violets, coleus, bloodleaf, baby's tears, oxalis, patience plant, pilea, prayer plant and peperomia.

Consider planting a tropical terrarium. The stage: a pebbly, shell-strewn beach, as restful as a faraway island paradise. The plantings: a luxurious tropical assortment of foliage plants, such as palms, Cyperus, philodendron, Aglaonema, Schefflera, sensitive plant, Zebrina, Chlorophytum, Syngonium.

If you set a terrarium in a window, with light behind it, filigreed plants with a strong silhouette, such as ferns, will be tremendously effective. If, on the other hand, your locale is a table, or anywhere that receives its primary lighting from overhead, you'll want to stress plants whose most striking claim to attention is their texture.

In Victorian days, you recall, the standard terrarium displays that adorned conservatories and parlors were the Wardian cases, chiefly filled with ferns. They were free-standing, constructed of ornately decorated iron frames supporting the sheets of glass. A contemporary version, relatively easy to plan, would be a terrarium wall. You could utilize a bookcase, a room divider or a recessed window nook as the setting into which the framework for the glass could be built.

4.

HOW TO PLANT: *Tanks,*

Bottles and Bowls

This is a simple how-to-plant-it chapter, exploring the up-to-your-elbows expanse of the tank planter; the intricacies of the bottle, with special emphasis on the narrow opening—and the keep-your-hand-in variety of planter such as the brandy snifter or fishbowl, both non-oblong containers that combine easy access with great visual appeal.

One preliminary remark that applies to all categories of glass gardens: whatever the size or shape of your chosen terrarium, make certain that you start (and finish) with glass that's spotlessly clean. Concentrate on the *inside;* smudges, fingerprints and other outside marks are easily removed after you've finished. Use glass wax or window spray for flat surfaces; as for brandy snifters and bottles, any detergent containing ammonia will make them sparkle, as will the dishwasher if you have one. If you've lost your heart to an old medicine bottle that retains interior stain, soak it out with Clorox. In addition, you may need to scrape it out, assiduously, with a perco-lator brush.

If you've got a hand-sized opening or larger, dry out the terrarium interior with a lint-free cloth. In the case of narrow-necked bottles, shake out the water, tilt them downwards in a warm place, and let them dry in their own time.

Repeated reference is made in this chapter to such things as soil, gravel, charcoal, sphagnum and moss, all of which are discussed at much greater length later on. But each of these items can be purchased at greenhouses, nurseries, garden centers and other sources of supply; all-purpose soil, which does for most plantings, is for sale in department stores, supermarkets, etc. You'll find a detailed dissertation on soil and planting media in chapter 5.

PLANTING THE TANK TERRARIUM

The advantages of the oblong planter are evident. Rectangular planters are glass gardens unlimited. You've ample scope for exercising gardening originality and whim. You can pile in the rocks as you see fit, without the intrusion of spatial consideration and the exacting demands of the narrow orifice.

A PREVIEW OF WHAT YOU'LL DO

1. Line the container with moss, the green side pressing against the glass, and secrete bits of charcoal in it. 2. Spread gravel over the bottom surface for drainage. 3. Add soil in proportion either to the size of the container or to the height of the vegetation; specifics follow. 4. Plant trees and taller background material first, filling in afterward with medium-sized ferns and low creeping growth. 5. Cover roots carefully with soil, which can in turn be concealed under bits of moss. 6. Water the garden thoroughly; cover it. 7. Put the newly-planted garden in a cool, sunless place for several days, as this will give the plants the time they need to adjust to their new surroundings. 8. Then, move your glass garden to a *light but not sunny site,* relax, and watch it grow. You'll have to take the cover off from time to time if moisture condenses unduly (see chapter 5 for maintenance, care, and danger signals)—but other things being equal, the garden should take moderately good care of itself.

WHAT YOU'LL NEED

You'll need moss, gravel, soil, charcoal; your plants; whatever rocks, pebbles and other landscaping ornaments you have in mind; tools.

For oblong terrariums and other relatively roomy planters, any of the smaller trowels and/or hand tools are usable. Trowel-and-rake combinations are useful if you can find them, but children's miniature gardening sets are more readily come by. I myself rely, for most planting chores, on a simple tablespoon! Have a scissors on hand for pruning and moss-cutting; be on the lookout for useful planting gadgets in gift and nursery catalogs, in hardware stores, and at toy counters. The strangest items may come in handy. If you're planting a desert terrarium with prickly cactus, use kitchen tongs, perhaps the most useful of all all-purpose gadgets and available for less than fifty cents. If you've misplaced the tongs, try a clamp clothespin for placing a pad-type cactus.

PLAY-BY-PLAY

Moss

Song for a terrarium-tiller: "Look for the Mossy Lining." You *can* pour soil directly into the container, but a moss liner, besides its obvious attractiveness, does soak up moisture and prevents the glass from becoming muddy. So line the terrarium with moss (see Sources of Supply). If it's dried decorator moss you're using, freshen it first in water and drain it well before you insert it. My own preference is for living sheet moss. (See "Moss" under "Woodland Plants," chapter 12, Plant Encyclopedia.)

The *bottoms* of oblong planters do not need to be lined, although in the case of certain plants such as the carnivores (see Plant Encyclopedia, "Houseplants") whose growing medium is moss rather than soil, you'll certainly want to do so. Also, you won't want to put much moss, if any, along the front, or viewing side, of your container, as this is the low foreground part of the vista and you don't want to obstruct the view. So, with your scissors, cut moss strips that measure the length and width of the terrarium, and insert them along the back and the two sides. (If you're a confident moss-manipulator, cut a single strip the length of the back plus two sides, and insert it in one piece.) The height of your liner will vary, of course, with the depth of the soil, which in turn can vary from one (you may want one inch of liner along the front, depending on your design) to many inches. If there's a hillside in your garden plan, the moss liner must be extended sufficiently to cover the bulge and allow for the added height. *Overlap the moss strips* so that the soil won't spill through any gaps. If you do decide to line the floor as well, you can insert that portion of the liner in one piece.

Soil

Proper soil and adequate rooting space are your primary concern;

at the same time, the growing medium (soil/gravel) is the visible earth of your creation, and should be attractively proportioned to the height of your terrarium and to your planted world inside. As you acquire a practiced eye, you'll be able to appraise a container at a glance, and to estimate the precise amount of soil needed, sufficient for supporting plant growth. The general rule of 1 to 4 holds: 2½ inches for a 10-inch-high terrarium; 5 inches for a tank 20 inches high, etc. Include gravel, my own formula being approximately ⅛ inch as part of every 1 inch of soil.

Plants

Actually, the planting of a roomy, tank variety of terrarium has much in common with outdoor gardening. Leave as much soil on the roots of your plants as space permits. Now, set the plant at the same depth at which it was growing before; the top of the root ball should be level with the soil surface. On dry rooted trees and woody plants, the division between stem and underground trunk is indicated by the lighter bark of the stem (aboveground area). Ferns are planted with their crowns set slightly above the soil.

Watering

The rule is: lightly but thoroughly, using a rubber hand sprayer. Make certain that the roots of your plants are adequately moist by probing with your finger. (See section on "Watering" in chapter 5.)

Cleaning

Size permitting, you can wipe off mud stains and moss flecks with a lint-free cloth. To get behind plants that are pressing against the glass, use a vegetable brush. Finger marks on the outside of the glass blur the garden vista as though you were seeing it through soiled eyeglasses: wipe them off with a treated cloth, or with window cleaner.

Covering the container

Your cover must fit snugly. Seal any gaps with transparent tape. Do *not* use a permanent sealant as you'll want to take off the lid to ventilate or to transplant or to make repairs. Plastic must be stretched tightly and taped. A large terrarium may require several panes of glass for covering.

Planting plan for 5-gallon tank planter 12 inches high, 12½ inches wide, 24 inches long; 3 inches of soil and drainage gravel.

Procedure: *Insert moss liner, 3 inches high at rear and sides, lower in front; fill with soil and gravel. Add accessories and plants as follows: 1-7: rocks; place these first. 8: steps; small flat stones pressed into background soil. 9: stepping stones. 10: fence. 11: pool, a shallow saucer pressed into soil. 12: sensitive fern. 13: wood fern. 14: pachysandra. 15: umbrella palm. 16: living sphagnum. 17: Christmas fern. 18: violet. 19: green plant. 20: living sphagnum. 21: ajuga. 22: lichen and moss strips. 23: fern. 24: tuft of grass. 25: ajuga. 26: creeping loosestrife. 27: hemlock. 28: coleus. 29: ajuga. 31, 32: gravel patch. 33: lichen-covered bark. 34: gnarled driftwood branch. 35: weatherworn root. 36: figurine.*

PLANTING THE NARROW-NECKED BOTTLE

Bottle gardens offer a challenge of their own, and your prime weapon for meeting it is patience. You'll do well to postpone work on your bottle garden if you are in a hurry to make dinner, keep an appointment, or in a frazzled condition for any reason. Bottle gardening is a *leisure occupation,* geared to relaxation and highly resistant to tension. Now, assuming peace is with us, let's take to the bottle.

A RESUME OF WHAT YOU'LL DO

1. Insert your moss, either in pieces or in small wads depending on the size of the opening. 2. Add gravel. 3. Pour in soil. 4. Put in your plants, with both before-and-after pruning required. 5. Add charcoal. 6. Clean up the bottle. 7. Water, or sprinkle, lightly. 8. Insert the cork or stopper—and you're in business.

WHAT YOU'LL NEED

Moss; gravel; soil; charcoal; plants; pebbles (optional); tools. You can master the insertion and transplanting of the trickiest bottle plantings with just a few simple tools. The ideal bottle planting tool

A toolkit for bottle plantings (below).
(Drawings on opposite page). You can make a long-handled conveyor from a wire coat hanger with a loop at the bottom to hold the plants. With a dowel, poke the plant out of the loop into the mossy niche at the bottom of the bottle.

should measure a few inches longer than the height of the container, so that you can keep matters firmly in hand, and not risk losing your plant somewhere inside. Here is your suggested toolkit for bottle plantings:

Dowels: a dowel, whittled to a point at one end, is the best all-purpose bottle-planting tool you can find. There is a dowel size for almost every bottle opening, ranging from a fraction of an inch to several inches in diameter. *Wires:* Cut yourself a length from a wire hanger. For snaring, bend it into a hook. *Miscellaneous:* orange sticks, ice-picks, chopsticks, pickle forks, hairpins, iced-tea spoons. (Note: for giant mineral bottles, work with long-handled spatulas, spoon and barbecue forks. Wire them to dowels for added length if needed.)

For Pruning and Trimming:

Use scissors. Long-handled surgical and pronged retractable olive forks, if you can find them (bar and cocktail supply places some-times have them), are fine trimming tools for bottle interiors. For breaking and snaring unwanted foliage, use wires bent into hooks.

For Watering:

Rubber hand sprayer.

For Conveying Soil and Gravel:

A plastic cylinder or tube that you can fit into a funnel. This could be a converted toothbrush container, or any similar plastic packaging item that's in the form of a tube. Seek, and you'll find. For angling gravel or a small pebble just right, try a plastic straw or, a family discovery that I myself am never without, a peashooter.

For Cleaning:

A percolator brush and the versatile pipe-cleaner.

Enlarge this introductory assortment to suit your particular needs; you'll probably unearth several special working aids of your own. Remember that discovery lies ever ahead of us, and the perfect all-purpose, combination poking-planting-filling-trimming-and-removing tool has yet to be patented.

HOW TO PLANT A NARROW-NECKED BOTTLE.
Lay the moss liner. *Cut a block of moss 2 inches larger than the base of the bottle. Because the neck is so narrow, cut the moss into pieces small enough to poke inside and patch together on bottom with a stick. Press green side outward against the glass.* Add the soil. *Funnel in ¼ inch of drainage gravel, tap 2 inches of dry powdered soil through beverage funnel inserted into a plastic straw or other tube. Add several bits of charcoal too, either now or after planting is finished, to keep soil from smelling sour.* Plant. *With a stick several inches longer than the height of the bottle, poke largest plant in first, leading with the root. Then insert the smaller wood fern.*

Accent with gravel. *A decorative patch of aquarium gravel accents the greenery. Tap it through funnel and tube, placing patches neatly wherever you want them.* Water. *Spray the planting lightly with a rubber hand sprinkler.* Clean the glass. *Use a percolator brush, and bend the wire to get at the curves. Now cork the bottle,* et voila.

The finished product: *This old-fashioned, quart-sized medicine bottle is 8 inches tall, and its opening is ½ inch in diameter (less than the size of a dime). The garden inside features a 6-inch chlorophytum and a 3-inch wood fern, planted in 2 inches of soil and gravel.*

And, having written that sentence, I must retract it, at least in part. Just as this book goes to press, I've been apprised of the following terrarium godsend: *a flexible mechanical finger,* 17½ inches long, for removing undesirable foliage and other objects from the bottom of bottles. A plunger activates two spring steel gripper jaws at the end of a flexible shaft that can be bent or held in an "S" or right-angled position. (See Sources of Supply.)

PLAY-BY-PLAY

Moss

You'll put moss in first, as a lining, but the amount of moss you'll need is determined by the amount of soil required. So here is a simple rule-of-thumb table giving approximate soil depths:

Inches of soil (gravel included)	*Height of bottle*
1½	5
2½	10
3	12
6	24

You'll see that you want approximately ¼-inch growing medium for every inch of bottle. And in calculating the size of your liner, remember that if you propose a slope or a hill somewhere in the bottle landscape, you'll want to accommodate the extra soil entailed. For example: in a 12-inch bottle with a 3-inch soil requirement, you may (even though only God can make a tree) elect to create a small mountainside 2 inches high. This will increase the soil height in one area to 5 inches. So make certain that you cut enough moss so that this extra 2 inches of soil will be lined.

Because you're working within the stringent limits of a small bottle opening, you'll need to cut the moss—or break it—into several segments—or into tiny wads small enough to push inside. Roll these fragmentary pieces into tight cylinders *with the green side out* so as to keep the bottle neck clean. Now, poke them through with the pointed end of your planting dowel. Piece them together, green side still looking out, pressed against the bottom and sides of the bottle. Continuing in this same fashion, add enough moss to accommodate your soil and to form a luxurious living carpet of greenery.

Remember that these patched bits and pieces *must overlap,* so that there are no gaps through which the soil can show. Press the moss firmly against the sides and bottom, but bear in mind that the liner won't fit snugly until it's been weighted down with what comes next: the soil and gravel.

If you're using sphagnum (live or shredded), insert it in small tufts, and pack it around the sides to the desired depth; you don't need to cover the bottom. Dried shredded sphagnum must be thoroughly moistened and squeezed nearly dry before you insert it.

Gravel

Never underestimate the importance of gravel. The fact that it doesn't show has no bearing on the importance of its role. If the bottle is to function as a self-contained unit, a layer of gravel is a *sine qua non:* even the shallowest drainage facilities will help to prevent soggy soil in overly moist containers. How much gravel you'll use will depend on the size of the bottle. I include drainage gravel in my estimate of the soil I'll need, allotting aproximately ⅛ of an inch for every 1 inch of soil. Thus, those 3 inches of soil we've calculated for a 12-inch bottle would incorporate ⅜ of an inch of gravel.

Use aquarium gravel for the narrow-necked bottle. Tap it into the moss cup through your plastic tube, straw or whatever you've fitted into your funnel. The gravel must be dry, or it'll clog. Spoon it into the funnel in small amounts. Using the blunt end of the dowel, spread it around inside the moss to the desired depth. Granted, this is largely a guesswork procedure, but as you aren't dealing with a precision machine part, a bit too much or too little won't knock the whole project out of orbit.

Soil

Funnel it, as you did the gravel, through your tube. The drier and more finely sifted it is, the easier it will pour. Cover the moss-and-gravel floor with it; make certain you fill 'er up to the required depth (approximately ¼ of the bottle's height).

Plants

Although anything small enough to fit into your bottle is fair game, you'll do well to choose young, small and slow-growing plants for your narrow-necked garden: transplanting and removing outsized plantings from these slender orifices is no joke. A wise preliminary caution, too, is to give all specimens an insecticide shower before you insert them.

If your plant has soil on its roots, retain it if possible, but if the soil is likely to smear the inside of the glass as you insert, wash the roots clean in advance. A root *ball* can actually be molded so as to clear the opening without soiling the sides of the container.

Now for the planting itself:

a. Prepare the way by making holes in the planting medium to receive the roots. Use the pointed end of the dowel.

b. Place your plant in the opening of the bottle, *root first*. (No breach births permitted.) It may look impossible to you; don't be discouraged. Do what pruning you can *before you insert* by measuring your bottle height and width (neck down, that is) against your specimens; still, you may have to do some root and leaf pruning before the plant slips through. If you must bend leaves in the course of this operation, *bend them upwards,* away from the root.

c. Poke the plant through the bottle neck by placing your smallest dowel against the thickest portion of the stem, just above the roots. Shake, tap the bottle, push, tilt, poke, pray, swear: anything goes, provided that you steer that plant into its appointed niche.

d. Using your dowel (or reasonable facsimile), cover the roots with soil and pack them as firmly as you can. Anchor unruly roots with pebbles (gravel) or wads of moss; pebbles and moss can also help you prop your plants upright.

Repeat this procedure until the bottle's fully populated and your design is complete. Quit while you're ahead (see "Bottle-planting Postscripts" below).

Charcoal

In the case of bottles, I prefer to add the charcoal *after* the plants and their roots have claimed whatever room they need. I secrete bits and pieces of it here and there in the moss with a dowel, where I can find room. If you prefer putting it in at the beginning with the moss, fine—but it may usurp a needed bit of planting space.

Added decor, optional

As limitations of size have ruled out such background interest as rocky landscaping, add a final accent, such as foliage, partridgeberry, or occasional gravel patches tapped through the funnel. As to pebbles: beware of a catastrophe in the narrow neck: either skip them, or measure carefully before tapping them through.

Now you're finished. Remove flecks of moss and mud with your percolator brush or pipecleaner. Water lightly with a rubber hand sprayer, and insert the stopper. You *did* it, by God! Your bottle garden's on its own.

BOTTLE-PLANTING POSTSCRIPTS

1. Don't overcrowd—better a few leftovers for another bottle garden than a cluttered planter. Also, take pains *not* to cross stems.

2. Don't use grass seed in a bottle. Forget it. You will not fancy the chore of snaring rebellious bits of grass through a bottle neck. Save the lawn for a tank.

3. Conceal your errors. If you've inserted a plant that proves to be a dislocated dud, and you can't snare it back up through the opening with your hooked wire, shove it into obscurity somewhere in the background. Use that great dissembler, moss, to cover up undesirable stones or miscalculated gravel patches. You'll soon become expert; meanwhile, be crafty.

4. If the shoulder part of the bottle surface eludes your attempts at brush-cleaning, twist several pipecleaners together in a crescent shape, wadding the ends of the crescent into balls. This scythe-shaped make-do can do the trick.

5. If your cork inadvertently slips through the neck into the garden, just treat it like a mistake: camouflage it with moss and call it a hillock. Or something.

VARIATIONS ON THE BOTTLE THEME

THE WIDER-NECKED BOTTLE OR ELONGATED JAR

Your approach to any vertical cylindrical planter will essentially be the one described just above. But for the many alluring bottle-type planters that don't fall into the narrow-necked category, note the following variations of procedure:

1. *Moss*

You can create a single liner as follows: Place your bottle on a suitably wide strip of moss. Measure a circle around the base of the bottle that extends beyond it exactly as many inches as the depth of your soil content (¼ the height of the container). For a planter 12 inches tall, cut a circle of moss that's 3 inches wider on all sides than the diameter of the bottle. Even though the moss will grow, cut the liner a fraction larger than your needs. (Scissors as usual.) And remember that if you're building yourself a hillside, calculate in the extra amount of moss needed to accommodate the additional soil.

If space permits, insert the liner as a single sheet. But it may bulge at the corners unless, prior to insertion, you make several small slits in the circumference. Thus cut, the liner should fit flat around bottom and sides. (Remember: *green side out.*) If you've got an intermediate-size opening, cut the lining in half, or even in quarters, and insert it piece by piece.

2. *Funneling Soil and Gravel*

With larger-mouthed containers, you can use a cardboard tube such as gift foil is wrapped around, or create your own hand-rolled cone from stiff paper or from aluminum foil.

THE LARGE WATER JUG

Tall, several-gallon water jugs enable you to grow larger plants in a spacious setting easily landscaped with long-handled tools. Increase the soil depth to meet the demand of more extended root systems. Soil and gravel are inserted through a cardboard tube; otherwise, proceed according to the instructions outlined above.

MINIATURES

The other extreme is always a conversation-piece, and a kind of wunderkind. Even a 1-inch bottle can house a seedling fern or several short-stemmed partridgeberries. Use the smallest tools you can find to fill these mini-planters. With a wire (such as a straightened-out paperclip given a hooked end with your pliers), poke in a tiny patch of moss; add a dash of gravel and a pinch of soil. Insert the plant(s) with a tweezer or stamp tongs; use a pencil, or lollypop or orange stick for ultra-narrow openings. Water with a medicine dropper and clean the inside of the glass with a pipe-cleaner, an ideal all-purpose gadget for miniatures.

Many of the plants listed in the encyclopedia are suitable for this kind of lilliputian-scaled glass gardening, provided you can find them small enough. Seedling conifers and ferns are always good subjects; so are bits of fern, which take on true fernlike proportions in the tiny

Just 1 inch of growing medium supports a 3-inch fern, already unfolding a new frond, in this 4-inch bottle.

bottle. Living sphagnum will look like conifer trees. Baby's tears, short-rooted lengths of Kenilworth ivy, partridgeberry and potato vine are all good creepers for confined surroundings.

The *Cladonia* lichens, which include the pixie cup and the red-tipped British soldier, are interesting subjects for small planters, but use them in such wide-mouthed containers as baby-food jars, because the clumps are brittle and aren't suitable for narrow-necked insertions. Also, if you plant these lichens, maintain them under slightly drier-than-average terrarium conditions, or they may mold.

PINCH BOTTLES AND HORIZONTAL PLANTERS

Tip the container on its side, as do those seasoned salts who patiently construct fantastic ship models inside of bottles. Your perspective changes accordingly: poke in the moss liner from the side, scale your soil content, not to the height of the planter but to its diameter, and add soil and gravel through a paper cone by tilting the bottle. Make certain, by the way, that the soil level is well *under* the level of the bottle aperture. The problem of handling a rounded bottle while you're working with it is solved by an egg carton, which will cradle the vessel nicely. Another home domestic solution!

Fill horizontally-viewed planters with low, sprawling plants such as strawberry begonia, partridgeberry, rattlesnake plantain, Zebrina, and Irish moss—the kind of plantings usually reserved for the low foreground of taller planters. Otherwise, the procedure is the same as for other bottle planting except that you'll be working in large part at a tilt. Tilt, by all means, when you water, so that the entire garden, both fore and aft, receives its share. Rounded bottles can be displayed on a wooden base to which they're anchored with modeling clay; neater, however, is the sawhorse effect obtained by nailing short crosspieces of wooden dowels together to form a pair of cradles.

HANGING PLANTERS

By and large, the glass used for these is delicate (see earlier chapter on containers). Accordingly, proceed with even more caution than usual. Minimize weight by going easy on the gravel, and by eliminating any and all stone accents. Cradle rounded bottoms in a bowl or small square box while you work, or things will be in a state of perpetual slither. Hang the bottle with picture wire wound tightly around the neck just below the lip. You're safe with any wire tested for 25 pounds, but my own preference is extremely fine, all-purpose hair wire, which, almost invisible, gives the impression that your hanging garden is floating in space. As to locale, consider suspending these spacesaving hanging gardens wherever they'll receive sufficient light. Several, hung at different heights, create a handsome effect. Make certain that they're set sufficiently apart from one another so that a passing breeze won't cause a shattering collision. Wine bottles with rounded bottoms are easily converted into hanging gardens.

BOTTLES FOR THE SINGLE PLANT

Display the symmetrical individuality of fern fronds and other sharply defined foliage in tall, tapered bottles. Set up a single bottle, or group several. If you are intrigued by leaf silhouettes, plant outstanding

A bottle with a glass stopper (left) holds a 5-inch Syngonium growing in 2 inches of moss-cupped soil. A 12-inch wine bottle (right) houses a delicately fronded wood fern planted in 3 inches of woodland soil, with ample head-room for growth. The soil is cupped in moss, and gravel is added for a decorative touch. This bottled fern will stay green all year round.

foliage in light-colored green or amber glass, illuminating them either by a window behind, or against a background of artificial light.

I predict that once you've hit the bottle, you'll become an addict. Far better to till than to tipple; if you acquire the habit, you'll want to try another, and then another, until you've conquered the narrowest bottle neck.

PLANTING A BRANDY SNIFTER OR FISHBOWL

Brandy snifters brimming with greenery are second in popularity only to the oval fishbowl which is planted in the same way—and you'll recall that you're likely to acquire a better grade of glass in the snifter. These long-stemmed planters offer the dual advantage of attractive design and plenty of planting room.

First, line the bottom of the snifter with moss ¼ the height of the

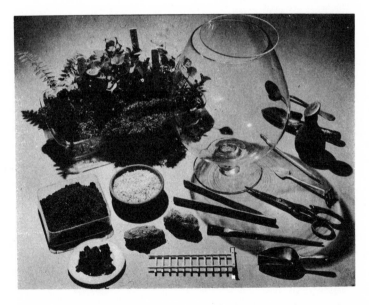

Ready to plant a brandy snifter. The fixings include a cover, plants, rich topsoil, small bits of charcoal to keep soil sweet, small stones, aquarium gravel, and miniature fence for landscape effect, and equipment for miniature garden making and maintenance.

Procedure: *1. Line one-quarter of brandy snifter with moss, green side out, or with damp sphagnum. 2. Add soil almost to edge of moss, with pieces of charcoal here and there, and place stones and gravel to produce interesting "terrain." 3. Set plants in place with small kitchen tongs (or whatever). This is the step where you'll strive for artistry as a "landscapist." Use a pencil and position plants attractively.*

glass. Slant the moss soil cup slightly upward and add the appropriate soil mixture which includes gravel and charcoal. Pack the soil firmly with your hand, sloping it upward against the correspondingly high portion of the moss liner. Following standard procedure, plant from the back, working down towards the lower foreground. Thanks to the abundance of working hand space, your use of temporary flowering plants is unlimited. Then cover the vessel with glass cut to the size of the opening, as described in chapter 2 on "Covers."

VI. LEFT: *On a shady patio, a 9-inch hanging planter suspended by hair wire is backed by a driftwood sculpture and a stucco wall. It holds wood fern and sprawling partridgeberry. Note the side pocket for planting; it can be sealed with tape or planted, in which case it must be watered about once each week to compensate for loss of moisture.*

VII. RIGHT: *A 5-gallon tank terrarium lined with moss (low in front and sloping upward at the rear) holds wax begonia, sensitive fern, coleus, living sphagnum, pachysandra, peperomia, chlorophytum, wood ferns, sprawling partridgeberry, rocks and gravel.*

VIII. LEFT: *Saikei landscape in a brandy snifter. A 7-inch sensitive fern and a 5-inch hemlock seedling occupy the raised rear. In the shallow foreground are a 3-inch clump of shining club moss and two 1-inch wood ferns. Rocks heighten the terrain and outline a dry central lake formed from white aquarium gravel. An arching bridge, a fisherman, the temple and lantern further the illusion.*

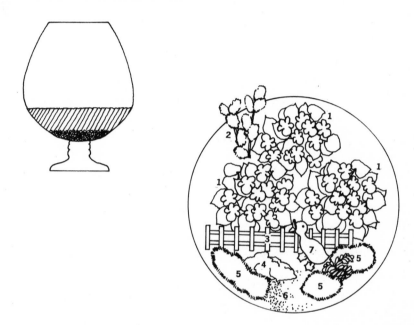

Planting plan for Color Plate IX (also shown on cover). Container and planting medium: *12-inch gallon brandy glass with 5¾-inch diameter, 9½-inch planting depth; 2⅛ inches of soil and gravel. Procedure: Insert moss liner; fill with soil and gravel. Then add plants as follows: 1, 3: budded viola plants; 2: pussy willow cuttings; 3: fence; 4: rocks; 5: wood fern and lichen; 6: gravel patch spread lightly in foreground; 7: figurine.*

IX. OPPOSITE: *Brandy snifter described on pages 64, 65.*

5.

AN ABC OF GLASS GARDEN
MAINTENANCE

With plant selection, planting techniques, arrangements and land-scapes partially behind you, you may now want to know more about why gardens in glass function as they do, and how best to keep them doing it.

Take time, then, to contemplate this little glass-enclosed world of your creation. This handful of air, soil and moisture is a self-contained unit capable of supporting vegetation for months, and even years.

As Dr. Ward learned a century ago, gardens in glass can flourish with little care. Even if you bypass many of the specific injunctions about soil, light, heat, watering and temperature that follow, your terrarium, with luck, should do nicely.

STANDARD OPERATING PROCEDURE

Here are a few basic primer-pointers on how to keep things going on a minimal basis:

1. Post-planting vigilance: Keep an occasional eye on your new garden for signs of malfunctioning, see 2 below. As suggested earlier, put it in a fairly light but not over-bright place for several days until the plants have settled in. You can then safely move the planter to stronger artificial or natural light.

2. These are the 5 salient terrarium distress signals:

Decaying foliage. This indicates excessive moisture. Remedy it by ventilation: open things up a bit. If your garden's in a narrow-necked bottle, you'll want to ventilate considerably longer than in the case of a tank or bowl, because air penetrates slowly through that small opening.

Stunted growth. This could be the result of improper soil; perhaps you're trying to rear alkaline-prone plants in too acid a soil, or vice versa: see, for example, the discussion on soil under "Ferns" in section 3 of the Plant Encyclopedia, and check individual plant requirements.

Yellow leaves. Another possible wrong-soil symptom. Or it could be inadequate drainage, in which case you'd refurbish the gravel supply; or insufficient air, simply remedied by ventilation.

Musty-smelling, moldy soil. Usually the result of poor drainage, this condition can be counteracted by adding gravel and also charcoal.

Brittle foliage and browned crisp moss. Thirsty! Give the garden a drink and review its watering needs.

3. If conditions are *too* favorable (as when your soil is too rich), plants may grow over-large and luxuriant. To maintain an orderly landscape, you must manicure. Break off and remove excess foliage; take out a plant that's outgrown its surroundings and put it someplace else.

4. If you've given the plants an insecticide bath before planting, you should have little trouble with insects, but we'll discuss these occasional pests later on. They may show up.

5. Disassembling: You have a choice. You may leave established planting undisturbed, adding new soil and moss seasonally. After pruning, cleaning and remodeling, a glass garden can look as good as, even better than, new. *However,* in some cases (you must judge this for yourself by looking and sniffing) it's a good idea to dismantle some gardens when warm weather takes over, because growth can become rank, and unsightly green algae may muddy up the moisture and cloud the glass. You can dismantle a bottle garden by washing, shaking and poking out the contents; then, wash out the bottle and allow it to dry, ready for the next go-round.

PRUNING, REMODELING AND TRANSPLANTING

How long does a glass garden last? You'll recall that Dr. Ward's famous original fern and grass grew for four years; he believed that plants could survive in glass for half a century. I've not been at it quite that long and so can neither confirm nor refute this estimate. However, I've kept terrariums growing successfully for several years, but not without repairing ravages caused by any given 6-month growing period.

Over a period of time, orderly landscapes may revert to a riot of untrammeled growth unless you trim overzealous plants: use a scissors in a large, accessible interior, and a hooked wire or a retractable olive fork for bottled foliage. Larger, easily gardened containers present no remodeling problems: prune out dead stems and foliage; add fresh soil, plants, moss and pebbles if and when needed.

Plants, we are agreed, do grow. Palms and other foliage that have outgrown their designated spots can be potted as houseplants. Conifers, ferns and other native plants, when they've gotten too big for their confines, should be set out in the garden late in the spring when the weather's grown sufficiently warm as not to imperil tender forced growth. (If you haven't got a garden, give them away to someone who has one.)

On the other hand, moss, at least in my experience, does not transplant readily out of doors. Store your salvageable moss, by all means, for reuse in the terrarium.

ERADICATING INSECT PESTS

The isolation of covered gardens generally immunizes them to most house-plant epidemics. Nevertheless, aphids and a few other breeds of insects are sometimes smuggled into the enclosed garden via moss and greenhouse plants. My own home remedy for aphids is tobacco smoke, an effective exterminating agent. But now there's a new aerosol type of general-purpose houseplant spray that can be directed through even the narrowest openings.

Try to direct the spray on the infested area only. Don't saturate the container; leave the cover off until fumes and spray have evaporated. Make certain to read the directions on the can carefully. Try to do your spraying in a relatively airy place (outdoors is ideal, but obviously impractical in the case of large tanks). Wipe the inside of the glass immediately after spraying; larger containers can be kept cleaner if you insert sheets of paper between plants and glass during the spraying process. In any case (literal and figurative!) don't leave unwiped spray on glass.

The following is a roll call of insect visitors you may expect in any given terrarium invasion:

Aphids head the list, as they thrive in moist humidity. They are less politely known as plant lice, and come in assorted shades of red, green, or black. Their presence is made known by a decline in the health of your plants' leaves, which first become sticky and shiny and then yellow; in any event, the clusters of these soft-bodied insects are easily seen.

Mealybugs look like shreds of cotton; if finger-insertion room permits, daub them with alcohol and they'll perish forthwith.

Mites cause brittle or undeveloped leaves and flowers. By their fruits shall ye know them. Get rid of them fast.

Red spiders are mercifully rare visitors to Terraria; they revel in hot dry air. But they do show once in a while.

White flies are persistent pests and may take several sprayings to remove.

Earthworms are by no means 100% malignant; they may, in fact, be the gardener's best friend, because they aerate and enrich the soil. But this very digestive action can be disturbing to terrarium plant roots confined to small areas. Telltale wormcast (a cylindrical mass of earth voided by earthworms) indicate that your plants are entertaining guests. Coax the worm to the surface at night by sprinkling lightly with lukewarm water and by scratching on the soil surface. Let him emerge in his entirety before you spear him, if he's in a bottle, or else catch him in your fingers (kinder fate for the worm) if space permits.

Scales are oval, shell-like objects difficult to detect on leaves and stems. Spraying will control immature scales, but once they're full-grown, you'll have to pry or brush them off with a wire.

Nematodes will cause plants to fail for no apparent reason: should such unaccountable decline befall some of your specimens, inspect the roots for nodules or lumps, the presence of which mean that nematodes are at work. Badly infected plants are best discarded entirely, unless the plant itself seems to be in generally good condition, in which case replanting it in fresh soil sometimes helps.

Insect eggs in woodland moss may explode the population of your glass garden if you collect your own moss. The resultant surprise assortment of insects will include some that are more entertaining than harmful. (Moss is not only a nursery for forest seedlings, but a depository for myriads of insect eggs. Often an entire generation is perpetuated in secret mossy places after the parents have succumbed to frost.) Among possible varieties of newly-hatched creatures are wire worms, mayflies, mosquitoes, spiders, sand fleas, crickets, katydids and grasshoppers. Take them in your stride. If they aren't disturbing the plants, leave them or release them. But a mosquito, pesky enough in July, is downright inadmissable at Christmas.

Katydids can decimate your garden is no time, bursting their skins at the expense of your landscape. One winter I watched several of these hatched insects defoliate a bottle planting into a wasteland. The supreme irony was that as I couldn't remove them from the bottle, I had to feed them after they'd devoured my last fern frond! Reverence for life, or downright lunacy?

WATERING

WHY

Briefly stated, the glass garden functions according to two basic cyclic principles:

1. Plants breathe carbon dioxide, formed by the oxidation of vegetable matter in the soil. They (the plants) then exhale oxygen, which is in turn incorporated by the vegetable matter.

2. Plants function further as a miniature rain forest, absorbing water from the soil which is then evaporated into the air. This evaporated water, when confined in a terrarium, can't dissolve into the atmosphere; therefore, it's condensed by the glass. Beadlike patches of moisture are formed which, like rain clouds, become heavy and then break, trickling down the sides of the glass like rain, to be absorbed by the soil. This process of evaporation and condensation is repeated in a continuing cycle.

This understood, you can see why you must water your garden before you seal on the cover—lightly, but thoroughly enough to get the rainmaking cycle functioning. I.e., wet the soil sufficiently to create the moisture which the plants must first absorb. *Water sparingly at first*. Underwatering is preferable to soggy soil. You can always add more water if it's needed, but excess moisture *must* be evaporated by ventilation; plants rot quickly in a sodden container.

I moisten the soil until the side moss darkens slightly, concentrating water on deeper-rooted plants.

WHAT KIND

If you use tap water, let it stand at room temperature for several hours. Ideally, rainwater should be used for African violets, carnivores, mosses and most woodland plants; it's their native beverage. And melted snow is another natural benefactor; it contains small amounts of ammonia, nitric acid and other growth-promoting elements. But I don't kid myself: unless you're a rural glass gardener, you'll probably be using the tap.

WITH WHAT

Use either a "Mist-Ifier" or a rubber hand-sprinkler (see Sources of Supply). Either of these will direct water, in precisely the required amount, to precisely the spot where you want it. *Don't* use a tilted glass; *don't* carry your portable garden to a faucet tap: both are

Three months after planting, an assortment of partridgeberry, rattlesnake plantain, shining club moss and tree club moss are flourishing in this drum-shaped airtight fish bowl. Not a drop of water has been added since the cover was sealed on.

unreliable. You'll get too much water, or not enough. Heed the advice of an old hand.

A new terrarium water-gadget that does an excellent job is the SYFONeX hand sprayer, now sold by several nurserymen listed in Sources of Supply. It is a plastic bottle sprayer, whose "gun"-type top adjusts easily to a mist or jet stream. This top is also available as a separate unit that can be fitted to a beverage bottle. Recommended for the gadget-minded buff.

AFTERMATH

After the initial post-planting sprinkling, the garden is on its own. If the inside of the glass continues to be beaded with moisture, you'll know that all's well, and further watering is unnecessary: the rain-making cycle is underway. Water only when crisp moss and brittle foliage indicate the need. Perhaps you didn't water the newly planted garden enough; perhaps the moisture escaped because the cover wasn't sealed tightly.

The obvious danger signals of an overwet garden are: extreme moisture that clouds the glass; decayed foliage; saturated moss. Remedy the situation by propping up the cover slightly, or even removing it entirely until the contents dry out to normal moisture conditions.

You are wondering, of course, about uncovered containers, which we've advocated for a variety of plantings, specifically cacti and succulents. Obviously, you must water open plants in an unsealed glass garden more or less as you would other potted plants. But because there are no drainage outlets, water rather less heavily: you don't want to drench the roots. Frequent but light wettings are in order.

TEMPERATURE

An average daytime room temperature in the high sixties or low seventies is satisfactory for most terrarium subjects, although certain houseplants and woodland plants prefer it on the cooler side. (For individual imperatives, see the Plant Encyclopedia.) Bottled atmosphere, unless it's warmed by the sun, whose natural heat is greatly augmented by glass, differs little from that in the surrounding rooms. The glass walls do create a special environment, however; they serve as protective insulation from drafts, and prevent chilling from sudden temperature drops. They act, in a word, as self-regulating incubators. And, although glass gardens will cool off at night, a temperature drop that plummets as low as 60° F. won't damage the plant inhabitants, not even the tropicals. Quite the contrary: not only is the life of the flowers' blossoms prolonged, but cooler night temperatures help the plants to assimilate whatever food matter they've taken in during the day.

My largest terrarium planter contains a gregarious plant assortment. It stands in my bedroom window, which I open every night regardless of the weather. Thanks to the adaptability of this hardy garden, I can indulge my craving for nocturnal fresh air without endangering my glass-dwellers' health—but this treatment isn't recommended for more delicate vegetation.

Among the plants with special temperature requirements, most of which are given in the Plant Encyclopedia, are arbutus, violets, violas, African violets, fibrous begonias, lilies-of-the-valley, cacti-succulents in covered containers, orchids, and carnivorous plants. (Note that small bulbs, which bloom out of doors in the early spring, will thrive in low temperatures of 40° to 50°.)

So that you can arrange compatible plant groupings and cater to their (by and large) not-very-demanding climatic inclinations, here are the majority of plants you're likely to deal with, grouped in accordance with their temperature needs.

COOL TEMPERATURE PLANTS (55° to 65°)

The cool temperature plants include the hardy native evergreen species, or plants that flower early in the spring such as the trailing arbutus and the viola. Mosses and lichens can survive sub-zero cold; at the same time, they stay lush and green in torrid summer heat. Use them, by all means, with the cool temperature plants for lining terrariums, and with any plant grouping as garden fillers.

Most of the plants in this group react favorably to average household temperatures *provided they aren't exposed to direct heat.* Suggested cool sites are cold windowsills, attics, basements, garages, unheated sun porches, or anyplace that provides abundant light, and where the temperature doesn't drop below freezing at night.

House and garden plants

aloe	onion
baby's tears	pachysandra
box	periwinkle
clover	Primula
conifers	silk oak
crassula	shamrock
cress	snake plant
Haworthia	viola
mushroom	violet
Norfolk Island pine	

Woodland plants

club moss	shinleaf
early Saxifrage	snowberry
goldthread	spotted wintergreen
hardy ferns	spring beauty (*Claytonia*)
liverleaf (*Hepatica*)	trailing arbutus
mosses and lichens	twinberry
princess pine pipsissewa	woodland violet
rattlesnake plantain	wintergreen

MEDIUM TEMPERATURE PLANTS (65° to 75°)

This group comprises the vast company of prime terrarium-dwellers, a compatible group that thrives in average indoor room temperature, including a nightly drop of about 10°.

African violet	coleus
aluminum plant	corn plant
aquatic plants	croton
Aralia	Echeveria
asparagus fern	grape ivy
Bertolonia	green plant
bloodleaf	inch plant
bugleweed (*Ajuga*)	Kenilworth ivy
cactus	leopard plant
Chinese evergreen	lily-of-the-valley

Nephthytis	prayer plant
orchids	Sedum acre
Oxalis	Selaginella
palm	Sempervivum
patience plant	Syngonium
Philodendron	umbrella palm
pick-a-back plant	strawberry begonia
potato vine	water lily
Pothos	Zebrina

Also in this group are the following woodland plants, which flower and leaf later in the spring, when the temperature has risen to this same 65° to 75° warmth:

deciduous ferns	lady's slipper orchid
foamflower	Solomon's seal
Indian ginger	trillium

WARM TEMPERATURE PLANTS (75° to 85°)

The smallest group of terrarium candidates are those plants that respond favorably to greater warmth, and to such sites as kitchens, bathrooms and locations near heating outlets, where the night temperature seldom dips below 65°.

butterwort	peperomia
caladium	pitcher plant
carnivores	velvet plant
Darlingtonia	Venus's flytrap
dumb cane (Dieffenbachia)	water hyacinth

SOIL

An introductory word to the concrete-bound city dweller or the suburbanite who may be put off by all that follows in this essay on soils and other planting medium components. Fear not. As I mentioned earlier, you can buy sterilized houseplant (all-purpose) soil at supermarkets, hardware stores, five and dimes, etc., all packaged in various quantities for your home use. And, with the addition of sand and charcoal, most of these pre-mixed compositions are suitable for terrarium plants. You can also buy special woodland soil for native plants, as well as African violet, cacti-succulent, and acid soil mixes. So, even if miles of concrete separate you from the nearest bona fide patch of dirt, you can still set up your terrarium.

Another thing. You will find, in various parts of this book, a good many directives about soil and soil mixtures. Plants certainly do have their soil preferences, formed, of course, by their normal native habitats, and the more you cater to them, the better they're likely to perform. But, *but*: plants, like people, are also adaptable. And although it may detract somewhat from the mystique of this book, I'm honor-bound to tell you that even those plants listed as having specific soil needs may surprise you by doing nicely in ordinary all-purpose terrarium soil, given acceptable drainage, light and a green thumb. Of course you should try to provide plants with their best growing medium, but I refuse to predict disaster for your terrarium-dwellers if you don't heed my every soil injunction. Nevertheless, what follows is in no way hot air, and it should be interesting and helpful. Or so I hope.

Proper soil is, of course, the prime ingredient for success in plant-growing of any kind. The soil used must contain all of the necessary nutrients, but too-rich mixtures will only stimulate excessive plant growth, and instead of a garden, you'll find yourself with a jungle. (And a jungle in a bottle spells ruin.) Well-balanced terrarium soils retain moisture, yet they're sufficiently porous to assure good drainage.

The diverse soils from which plants generate food are composed of various minerals. Some of the essentials are nitrogen, phosphorus and potassium, but lesser-known minerals, which are called trace elements, play equally vital roles in maintaining a plant's wellbeing. A deficiency in one or several of these could be detrimental to proper plant development.

It is important that you know a given plant's soil preference, not merely for the nurturing of that particular plant, but so that you can plan compatible group plantings. Whenever it's possible, grow your plants in their indigenous soil. Sphagnum bogs and conifer forests are the natural haunts of acid-loving plants. Lesser degrees of acidity are found in oak woods, or in the soil around rotting stumps and in sandy pine barrens. Alkaline-prone vegetation favors limestone outcroppings, coastal salt marshes, and desert areas. You can meet the needs of acid-feeding plants by obtaining soil dug in the vicinity of oak or apple trees. An alternative is to add some peat to your soil composition. Desert cactus and other alkaline plants will benefit from a handful of powdered lime. You see, your soil can be doctored. Most plants aren't too fussy and will grow in soil that's neutral, or slightly acid or alkaline.

THE GROWING MEDIUM: TYPES OF SOIL AND OTHER COMPONENTS

Don't prepare soil mixtures until you familiarize yourself with some of the ingredients that you'll be using.

Loam is another name for topsoil; it's composed of clay, silt and sand in varying degrees; one speaks of sandy or clay loam, depending on the composition.

Humus is decayed vegetable matter of different kinds. What's referred to as leaf mold is, more specifically, decomposed woodland humus. Old decayed stumps are a prime source of humus.

Sphagnum, or *peat moss,* are one and the same, despite general confusion on the subject. Regardless of the label, the genus *Sphagnum* comprises all the various species of peat moss. They're all bog mosses, and commercial peat is dug from ancient sphagnum bogs. You can obtain two varieties:

Shredded sphagnum is highly absorbent. It's invaluable for transplanting seedlings and for filling gaps in terrarium landscapes. Its light-green color makes an attractive color contrast with the darker mosses used for linings. Roots that are packed with sphagnum are assured of proper aeration, of perfect drainage, and of receiving ample amounts of soluble plant food. Use it.

Milled sphagnum is refined moss, as finely textured as sifted soil from which the acidity has been baked out. (See Sources of Supply.)

Vermiculite is a mica by-product, expanded by heat into spongy resilient particles to add porosity to soil composition and prevent packing. Sterile vermiculite is beneficial to the rooting of cuttings, but as it lacks nutrients, the plants must be fed frequently. Finely textured vermiculite is best for rooting; the coarser variety is the kind you'll want to incorporate into soil mixes.

Sand is a clean builder, provides drainage in planting mediums, and acts as a firm base for rooting cuttings. If you live, as I do, near the seacoast, you'll be tempted to use beach sand, but don't succumb: salt is toxic to most plants. Repeated washings won't help; it's impossible to remove completely the salt crystals with which it's impregnated.

Gravel is the terrarium gardener's general aid and accessory; it supplies drainage and bottom moisture; in various forms, it's used for terrarium accents and landscaping. Aquarium gravel offers good drainage and is easily tapped through a funnel. It's available in many colors, but white is my own preference for garden accents. Green and other shades, however, may be more harmonious with dried arrangements. Pebbles and stone chips are useful for larger garden displays; they retain bottom moisture in display terrariums of potted plants. Garden suppliers sell ready-to-use pebble packages, but builders' gravel must be washed before you use it.

Charcoal, formed by airless slow burning, which permits gases to escape, is a form of carbon that's used in terrariums for the purpose of absorbing soil impurities. Crushed charcoal contributes to soil porosity and, in addition, if used as a preventative, will keep moist terrarium interiors sweet-smelling. A handful of charcoal pieces, inserted in the moss lining and amongst the gravel, can spell the difference between the fresh, damp, pleasant scent of growing things and a rancid-smelling swamp.

MIXING ALL-PURPOSE SOIL

If you're doing it yourself, blend your soil as carefully as though you were mixing a cake. If you leave out vital ingredients and compose this basic mixture carelessly, your plantings will turn out as unsatisfactory as your cake would under similar conditions of negligence.

Basically, the peatmold-loam-sand mixture prescribed by Dr. Ward for his first bottle planters remains a reliably sound formula. For an all-purpose terrarium soil, take two parts topsoil to one part sand; add milled sphagnum and leaf mold. Vermiculite is optional but (see above) it has much to recommend it, especially for ensuring sturdy root growth.

A list of specific soil recommendations is found under the headings of the individual plants in the Plant Encyclopedia.

FERTILIZERS AND AUXILIARY PLANT FOOD

In the section on "Maintenance and Care" above, you recall my stating that over-rich soil would bring about excesseive plant growth. Healthy plants should be maintained with proper soil and environment; by and large, don't encourage growth by auxiliary feeding. Feed only slow-growing plants, and those that can be conveniently removed without disrupting the entire garden. The warm humidity that is the terrarium's special province itself accelerates plant growth. I generally limit feeding to a sprinkling of slow-acting bone meal (and this only in larger planters, where trimming, replacing, and population explosion don't pose insoluble problems) or to a general-purpose soluble fertilizer, so labeled by the manufacturer. Specific feeding needs for plants such as cacti and succulents, carnivores and others, are detailed in the Plant Encyclopedia. In any case, if your soil is dry, water before you feed: it will aid the absorption process.

LIGHT

Light is as essential to plant growth as are proper soil, warmth, and abundant moisture. Buds need a daily diet of light-hours before they can blossom. These hours can vary by minutes, but must be steady and uninterrupted, or the energy-packed light rays are wasted.

Plants vary as to their light requirements much as they do with regard to temperature. Summer-blooming plants require long days; shorter-day plants flower in reduced light during a far briefer light span. In the neutral category fall many of our familiar houseplants, such as wax begonias and African violets, which flower the year round.

That trusty repository of useful wisdom, the Farmer's Almanac, informs us that the longest stretch of consecutive daylight during any given 24-hour cycle is 15 hours and 19 minutes, and it occurs at the time of the summer solstice, in June. By contrast, December's low is 9 hours and 6 minutes—a hefty differential. The cycle, as it alters, brings about some heart-lifting surprises: I've often been delighted to find violets blooming in my woods during the late autumn! Normally plants that open during the shorter days of early spring, they mysteriously missed their appointed debuts, and the tardy buds developed and opened during the autumnal days of a corresponding light span.

The eccentricities are limitless: many native plants such as partridgeberry and pipsissewa flower in dense summer shade; yet they encounter considerably lighter conditions during the winter, when bright but mild sunlight penetrates the leafless winter woods. Many of these so-called sunless plants and deep-shade growers are, therefore, tolerant of several or more hours of weaker winter sunlight.

NATURAL LIGHT

Have a look at your exposures in terms of where your windows are situated, and note the following fairly obvious rules-of-thumb: *North-*

Show off your potted plants in a spacious, artificially-lit climatically controlled plantarium. This display includes azaleas, African violets, cyclamen, and wax begonias on a base of white pebbles.

northeast windows are relatively sunless, but light enough so that most mosses, ferns and foliage plants (the staple plants of terrarium gardens) will flourish in their vicinity. *South-southeast* windows offer the best exposure for blossom bowls and for tropical flowering plants. However, you can also grow shade-loving woodland and foliage plants in these southerly-light windows if you provide some shading device, such as a Venetian or slatted bamboo blind. *West-southwest* windows bear the full brunt of the afternoon sun, and space receiving this bright exposure should be reserved for the sun-hungry carnivores, desert cacti and succulents, and miniature water lilies.

But the fact is that you can accommodate any terrarium plant in any window, whatever its exposure, provided that there is enough light and that you filter and diminish the sun's heat and light through blinds and draperies.

Red Light: Danger Signals

If the leaves of foliage plants turn yellow or develop burnt edges, it's possible that they're receiving too much sunlight. If moisture builds up heavily in the terrarium, it could be from the same cause. Cure: Give shade, and in the case of excessive moisture, ventilate as suggested above.

Tropism, or an unbalanced growth to one side, is bound to occur in plants growing by a window: they'll lean toward the source of light. This turning process is caused by swelling cells in that part of the plant *not* exposed to the window, which action bends the plant toward the light. It can be corrected in one of two ways: in the case of bowls or bottles, an occasional half-turn will maintain a proper balance; larger tanks can be given a once-in-a-while about-face, even though it means gazing at the rear of the background for a bleak day or two. (Extra-heavy tanks will reverse more easily if you set them on a strip of linoleum.) The other corrective is evenly distributed overhead light.

ARTIFICIAL LIGHT AND WINDOWLESS GLASS GARDENING

Thanks to the recent development of artificial lighting devices for terrarium use, you can pursue your hobby anywhere in the house, pitch-black (but airy) closets not excepted. Sunless bookshelves, interior windowless dining areas and gloomy basement corners can be converted into colorful growing areas. Fluorescent Gro-lamps, a brand new item, are both inexpensive and practical. You can set one up, complete with a 20-watt tube, for under 10 dollars; the cost of operating it 15 hours a day for a 7-day period will be about 5 cents, the most sensationally non-inflationary figure published this year. (By the time you read this, of course, the cost may have risen to 6 cents. You can still swing it.) Two 40-watt tubes burning over a similar period will average (at this writing) a mere 25 cents. You'll recall (see chapter 2, "Choosing a Container") that most of the hyper-equipped new cases such as Plantariums and Crystalite Greenhouses come equipped with fluorescent tubes.

Fluorescent desk lamps used for homes and offices provide about 20 watts, which might be adequate for some foliage plants, but I recommend two 40-watt fluorescent tubes for general use.

Because plants' light needs vary, I am giving groupings in three categories. In general, however, one can say that the average non-flowering terrarium plant needs just about 12 hours of light. (Annual seedlings that are being started in terrarium greenhouses, such as tomatoes, zinnias and marigolds, will need 15 hours of light to develop properly.)

Plants requiring high light. Place so that top of plant is about 6 inches from light source; keep lights on about 16 hours daily.

African violets	crassula
Aloe variegata	*Fatshedera lizei*
begonias (fibrous)	gloxinias
Codiaeum	impatiens
coleus	wax plant (*Hoya carnosa*)

Plants requiring medium light. Place so that top of plant is about 10 inches from light source; keep lights on about 14 hours daily.

aluminum plant (*Pilea cadieri*)   peperomia
anthurium   philodendrons
grape ivy (*Cissus*)   rubber plant (*Ficus elastica*)
Kentia palm   schefflera
   (*Kentia fosteriana*)

Plants requiring low light. Place so that top of plant is about 16 inches from light source; give light about 12 hours daily.

Chinese evergreen   *Philodendron oxycardium*
   (*Aglaonema simplex*)   snakeplant (*Sansevieria*)
Dieffenbachia (dumb cane)
dracaena
Nephthytis (*Syngonium*)

Yes, plants may be grown under artificial light without any exposure to natural light. However, this light must be as constant and uninterrupted as daylight, and also must terminate just as daylight does; let an electric timer do your thinking for you; remembering to turn lights on and off at specified hours can be a headache.

The use of artificial light can widen the scope of your terrariums' versatility: you may use them as centerpieces and decorative display in low-intensity light areas whenever you wish. Just give them an occasional 24-hour pickup under the fluorescents.

Fluorescent light won't burn foliage unless the bulb actually brushes against the plant. At close range, a strong incandescent bulb could burn tender seedlings, but plants covered with glass are less endangered by the proximity of electric light.

Lamps used above houseplants should stand between 1 and 2 feet above the top of the plant. In the case of flowering plants, however, the distance should be lessened: 10 inches is par for African violets for example; 6 inches for starting seeds. Obviously you'll decrease the intensity of the light by raising the lamps.

6.

TERRARIUMS IN BLOOM:

Twigs; Blossom Bowls;

Special Displays

With winter here, can spring be far behind? The slushy, dreary, grey weeks of latter February, March and even capricious April are surely the low point of the year for those of us with no available island in the sun; spring seems a dropout—a dead certainty never to reappear. I suggest a sure-fire tonic for these impatient weary days: blossom bowls of flowering plants and deciduous twigs, dug or cut from shrubbery in your garden, or acquired in other diverse ways. Easily forced in glass containers, these premature blossoms will lift your flagging spirits and carry you over the hump to that first unforgettable mild day when the fresh young down of Corot green first appears on the trees.

Many of these blossoms have that refreshingly elusive scent aptly termed "pale perfume" by Alice More Earle in *Old Time Gardens;* blended with the moist earthiness of the terrarium, it's the opulent smell of growing things. Lily-of-the-valley and cuttings of winter honeysuckle are prime purveyors of delectable floral scent.

FORCING BUDDED DECIDUOUS TWIGS IN GLASS

Even if you live in an apartment, you needn't be excluded from this intriguing form of glass gardening. And you don't have to sneak around, pilfering from the parks. Get forsythia and pussy willow cuttings for forcing from those few enterprising nurserymen who advertise them in the large city papers. Or buy surplus branches by the bundle, stick them in water, and refrigerate them until you want them. Yet another source of supply that's neither criminal nor costly to tap

84

are the stacks of branches left by tree-trimmers along the highway utility lines. Scavenge away.

Leading candidates for early floral forcing, because of their availability, their beauty and their quick-flowering propensities, are forsythia, pussy willow, and quince. Cherry blossoms, an erstwhile February favorite of my mother's, are more difficult to coerce prematurely today because of dry heated rooms: here's where the terrarium is an ideal fellow-conspirator. As cherry blossoms flower on shorter lengths of stem, they need less *lebensraum,* and a mere handful of twigs is all that's required for a colorful blossom bowl or for a presage-of-spring flowering in your terrarium landscape.

Stage your pre-seasonal display in any roomy bowl-shaped planter that you can cover easily. As most cuttings do require somewhat longer stems, you'll usually need an 8-inch container. For individual twigs, select a tall tapered bottle, provided the opening is large enough to permit easy insertion and removal. Try grouping several such bottles on a windowsill: their combined impact is more effective than any mixed bouquet.

WHAT TO CUT

Take cuttings only from trees whose buds were formed the previous autumn. Don't try to force shrubs such as Buddleia, roses, or hydrangea, all of which must produce buds on new spring wood. You'll have no trouble spotting the fall buds of forsythia, dogwood and flowering quince, but others are less conspicuous. Most flower buds are more rounded than the slender, tapering buds of leaves. Select only fully developed, heavily budded branches. Note that although apple blossoms are produced on older and darker wood, branches that are too old and unpruned should be avoided. Conversely, in the case of forsythia, it's newer growth that can be undesirable: don't cut the sparsely budded, light-hued forsythia canes.

WHEN TO CUT

You can cut deciduous twigs in January or even sooner, but cuttings taken this early will take longer to flower. I've found that by February, most early-flowering shrubs respond readily to forcing; having been fully exposed to freezing outdoor temperatures, the buds have had sufficient rest, and need only warmth and moisture to burst their scales. Forcing-time for all species narrows down to a very few weeks, and even days, as their normal outdoor flowering time approaches; branches cut at winter's end on a sunny day when the sap is running will open even more quickly.

The timetable for forcing twigs that follows is compiled from observations of cuttings made in my Connecticut garden, which corresponds, in our western coastal area, to Zone 7 on the United States Department of Agriculture Plant Hardiness Zone Map. Obviously, blossoming time varies with locale and environment. My own cuttings were, of course, from shrubbery growing near at hand. The list that follows can and should be enlarged to include satisfactory forcing materials in your own growing area.

Quick-Flowering Twigs

(2 weeks if cut in midwinter; 5 days in March): Forsythia, pussy willow, Andromeda (*Pieris japonica*), peach, barberry (Berberis), plum, cornelian (*Cornus mas*), alder (*Alnus*), birch (*Betula*).

Slower-Flowering Twigs

(6 weeks if cut in midwinter; 2 weeks or less in March and April): Apple, flowering crabapple, cherry, pear, dogwood, lilac, red maple, flowering quince (*Cydonia japonica*), Shadwood (Amelanchior).

Forcing twigs in a brandy bowl: forsythia, pussy willow and larch, with shorter lengths of andromeda blooming in the foreground. Count on about 10 days' duration for the forsythia; the others should bloom for 2 weeks. Cuttings made in midwinter should sprout leaf and blossom buds in about 10 days.

New Spring Leaves

(10 days to 2 weeks in midwinter). A few greening twigs in a Mason jar will lift your midwinter spirits far more than an entire verdant forest in May. My own favorite is the larch (*Larix laricina*), a deciduous conifer that may appear to be dead in winter. Close inspection, however, will reveal branches covered with woody knobs or spurlike buds that respond eagerly to the nurturing warmth of the glass garden. Cuttings of willow and choke cherry may also be forced for their foliage.

HOW TO CUT

Make a clean, slantwise cut with a sharp pruning shears to prevent injury to the shrubbery. Place the newly cut, frozen twigs in an unheated entryway as an interim step toward indoor warmth; then submerge them totally in cold water for 24 hours. If you've acquired your bundles of twigs by mail order, soak them for several days. You can increase the water intake and swell the growth cells by crushing and peeling the bark off the lower twig ends.

MEDIUMS FOR FORCING

Shredded sphagnum or aquarium gravel are your best bets. The required functions are only two: to supply moisture attractively, and to maintain a support for the twigs. No nutritional properties are entailed, because it is water, and water alone, that forces the buds to swell and open. Milled sphagnum and vermiculite become muddy, and are too light to support heavier branches. A moss or gravel base of several inches' depth is usually sufficient; conceal this basic support with a lining of living moss if you wish. And use charcoal—several large lumps of it.

TWIGS AS FILLERS

In the chapter on design, I made reference to the colorful contribution that quick-flowering cuttings can make to an established terrarium planter: concealed in moist moss, bare twigs pass unnoticed until they burst into abrupt blossom. A central mossy area reserved for forsythia cuttings, for example, will emerge as a spectacular focal area, come blooming time.

Twig addenda

Staminate alders and pussy willow catkins shed pollen when in full bloom, so place these cuttings where such pollen-shedding won't smear the glass. Willows root from the tiniest cuttings. Move them outdoors when the weather has warmed.

THE BLOSSOM BOWL

PLANNING AND PLACING

Your blossom bowl can be a radiant burst of individual color, or a mixed bouquet composed of several varieties of cuttings. Generally, a mixed arrangement should be restricted to those flowering twigs requiring similar timetables for forcing, or the end result will be patchy and spasmodic. Trim the twigs to the size of your bowl, grading them in height to suit yourself. Keep in mind the aesthetic law of no crowding, and leave ample room between your cuttings and the glass. Remove all dead growth, and give the ends another go-round of crushing and peeling. Insert the twigs deep enough into the container so that they'll stand upright, and so that the planting medium completely covers the ends. Finally, taking care not to disturb the arrangement, add water with a hand sprinkler. The moss or gravel base must be thoroughly saturated so as to satisfy the needs of thirsty twigs.

Flowering deciduous twigs can provide you with a continuous floral carnival from midwinter to May if you remove twigs that have had their day and replace them with fresh-budded plant material. Several blossom bowls started at strategic intervals will also assure you of a perrennially flowering centerpiece.

CARING FOR BLOSSOM BOWLS

Don't cover your blossom bowls tightly (except for arbutus, see below), as excessive humidity created by the wet moss may cause mold to form on the buds. If this starts to happen, remove the cover; if the moss then begins to dry out, simply add more water. (This is, admittedly, not Operation Negligence. Blossom bowls take caring for.)

These early spring blossoms need slow, cool forcing. Provide them with a dim room, with spring temperature of about 55° to 70°. Then, when the buds begin to color, introduce the bowls to increased light. The blossoms will last longer, however, if they're not exposed to direct sunlight after they come into bloom. And, too, you can prolong the flowering period (see "Violets" below) by popping the bowls into the refrigerator at night.

FLOWERING LANDSCAPES

Larger blossom bowls that include rocks, grassy lawns, moss patches and pebbly accents can be as spectacular as an outdoor landscape. For housing this kind of complex scene, tank planters are best. Follow the landscaping rules outlined in chapter 2, and then complete the procedure by adding, according to timetable, smaller quick-flowering twigs in the foreground. It's a lot of work; it's also a lot of fun; the effect, even if brief, is worth the trouble.

SOME STELLAR BLOOMS

Forsythia and Andromeda

These are among the most effective of the early spring blossom-bowl blooms. Golden bowls of forsythia are warmly welcomed attention-catchers wherever they're displayed. As for andromeda; think white, in graceful, sprawling racemes. Andromeda will flower in small containers from short 3-inch cuttings.

The Trailing Arbutus

Thanks to the terrarium, this celebrated bloom has finally shed its reputation for being difficult to grow. Indigenous to snowy spring woods, it responds favorably to cool moist covered containers. Remember that you should attempt to force only those plants that are already budded; you can easily locate the buds, formed the previous summer, at the ends of the trailing plants.

Start in the usual fashion by lining a spacious planter with sheet moss. Spread drainage gravel and charcoal bits on the floor of the container, and then fill in with *acid arbutus potting soil*. Soak the potted plants before you tap out the root ball. The longer, trailing plants that you've dug yourself must be wound about inside the con-

Brandy is dandy, but arbutus is prettier: Several 8-inch lengths of budded trailing arbutus are coiled about the container. The roots are poked into an acid soil mixture composed largely of rotted hemlock needles. Forced on a cool but bright window sill, buds begin to swell within 7 days and, in the winter months, usually flower during the second week. The fragrant waxen blossom clusters keep about 2 weeks—but the lifespan can be 2 months with refrigeration.

tainer, and the roots then poked into the soil. As for the budded cuttings that are the subject of this chapter, they'll root if you cover the ends with soil. Conceal such bare earthy spots as remain with either moss or a handful of hemlock needles. Finally, sprinkle the newly planted arbutus, and then place the bowls in a light but sunless place for several days. *Seal the cover tightly;* these plants thrive on humidity.

Budded arbutus will flower in about 2 weeks. When the buds are exposed to light and warmth, they'll begin to swell on about the 6th day. Most plants will start to make new growth within one month. Many of the flowers are followed by seed capsules, which resemble the flower of the starfish cactus. Given cool temperature, the waxen pink arbutus blossoms will last 10 days or longer, but their bloom can be prolonged by refrigeration.

Violets in Glass (see "Woodland Plants," Plant Encyclopedia)

If yellow ranks as the prime favorite among spring colors, surely the violet wins the favorite-spring-flower sweepstakes. You can force many kinds of violets both native and domestic, but I've been most successful with the rhizomatous (possessing root-like, subterraneous stems) species. The common *Viola papilionacea,* and *Viola affinis,* and the greyish-white large-flowered Confederate violet, *Viola priceana,* perform very well. I weed these riotous intruders from my flower beds by the bushel every summer, but they more than compensate for their estival nuisance value by the pleasure they provide in winter blossom bowls. The reason that these thick-rooted violets force easily is that, like flowering bulbs, they contain food energy that's activated by nothing more than warm, moist terrarium encouragement.

Include clumps of violets in your terrarium landscape plans, or enjoy them in blossom bowls, either multi-colored or predominantly purple. Press the knobby rootstocks lightly in the specified soil (see Plant Encyclopedia) which is cupped in moss with drainage gravel and charcoal. Cover the hairlike roots, but leave the eyes, from which leaves and flowers sprout, exposed. Plant fibrous rooted species with the stems at soil level, retaining a root ball whenever possible.

I find that violet rhizomes can generally be brought into flower within a month. I planted the roots of *Viola affinis* on January 1; buds appeared by the 24th and bloomed on the 29th. Other fibrous rooted violets may take 5 or 6 weeks to flower. Using prolonged refrigeration, I've preserved the flowering plants under glass for as long as 3 months!

If you try forcing unfamiliar violet species, research their individual preferences: not all of them are moisture-loving and sun-shy.

A 2-quart, 2½-inch fish bowl is housing a lovely catch of woodland violets, these being blue-grey Confederates (Viola pricaena) whose blossoms grow on 4-inch stems. The plump rhizome (see text) is pressed lightly into a soil composition of leafmold, sand and milled sphagnum spread to a depth of 1¾ inches over the bottom of the bowl.

Lily-of-the-Valley Pips

Fill a huge brandy glass with a dozen of these fragrant, bell-like blossoms. Or plant less, in containers that are smaller but equally tall. Spread about 2 inches of moss over the bottom, incorporating a few pieces of charcoal. The only acceptable planting material is shredded sphagnum. Pack moss around the roots; then, spreading the pips in your hand, place them in the bowl, and cover them with more moss until only the pinkish sprouts are exposed. The moss must be kept moist at all times, but never permitted to become soggy. Apply frequent mistings to buds in open planters. If the moss in covered containers becomes overly wet, ventilate from time to time. Keep the garden in cool darkness (50° to 65°) until the waxen yellow sprouts are four inches long. Then introduce it to subdued light until the sprouts turn green, and finally expose it to bright but not intensive sunlight until the buds begin to open. The flowers should last 10 days or longer at average room temperature. Forced florist's pips should be discarded after they've flowered. You can set up a dependable schedule of lily-of-the-valley blooms for special occasions by starting top-quality nursery pips 3 weeks in advance of your target date: for Thanksgiving bloom start on November 1; for Christmas, December 3, etc.

Primrose Bowls

Plant a primrose bowl by lifting plants from the garden or coldframe

Here's to your lilies-of-the-valley! Pack the roots of the specially-prepared pips in moist shredded sphagnum. When the sprouts are about 4" tall, shift them from shade and 50° to 65° to a sunny 70° window; they'll flower in about 21 days.

in early spring. Set them in a deep container of rich soil with ample drainage. The presence of cool temperature, partial shade and abundant moisture ensures success.

SPECIALTIES OF THE HOUSE:
SOME SHOW-OFF DISPLAYS FOR HOBBYISTS

ORCHIDS (see also Plant Encyclopedia, "Houseplants")

One of the first plants to immigrate to England in a Wardian case was a South American orchid; this prestige bloom thrives in the moist humid interiors of tank terrariums or plantariums. But orchids, as you might expect, are more demanding than the average terrarium habitant. Pot it in leafmold, fir bark, or fern fiber. As with the African violet below, ventilate. Don't close plantarium panels tightly; leave inch openings at either end of a covered terrarium. Avoid condensation of moisture in large drops. Spray the foliage on hot dry days, preferably in the afternoon. Promote beneficent moisture by pouring water on the gravel on which the plants are setting. And good luck to you.

AFRICAN VIOLETS (see also Plant Encyclopedia, "Houseplants")

You may want to show off individual beauties in bubble bowls, or to group several colors together in a large container. Or include them, as brilliant focal plantings, in your terrarium landscapes. The African violet thrives in glass because of the constant moist humidity. But use only new plants, because older ones will succumb to crown or stem rot in excessive humidity; place the plants so that they don't press against the glass itself, as this is where moisture collects. Be vigilant; ventilate frequently; don't let too much moisture accumulate.

MAKING A PARTRIDGEBERRY BOWL

I seem to revert to partridgeberries in every section of this book, my partiality dating, of course, from my aunt's bowls described in the foreword. These cheerful berried treasures, featuring the traditional Christmas colors, make every day a holiday. Line small glass bowls with moss, adding gravel and charcoal, then a thin layer of soil. Arrange short lengths of partridgeberry in layers, the fruit pressed against the glass, the group roots in the center of the bowl. When the glass is three-fourths full, cover the roots with more soil, and then insert a final upright layer of berries to create an all-around green and red ball of living color. Mist the plants before covering.

CUT FLOWERS IN GLASS CONTAINERS

Another string to your glass garden bow is an outstanding arrangement of a few cut flowers. Feature cuttings from your houseplants. Delight in the warmth of a geranium cluster, in the pastel softness of African violet blossoms. Revel in the solitary loveliness of a rosebud, or the first snowdrop of the newborn spring.

Old flowers will bloom anew in glass containers, so salvage the best blossoms from fading bouquets and corsages, too.

First, remove all crushed petals and foliage, and then trim the stems to container size. Add fresh fern fronds or evergreen cuttings. Put the flowers in needled holders and drop them into the container —gently, so that the weight of the holder won't shatter the glass. Tilt the container until the holder is in an upright position, and then cover it with aquarium gravel. (If the flowers are white, use colored gravel.) Add as much water as the stems will absorb. You can cover or not, as you choose, but a sealed container will retain moisture and keep the blossoms fresher. Again, refrigeration will contribute to the longevity of these bottled cut arrangements.

POTTED PLANTS IN SHOW-OFF TERRARIUMS

Glass gilds the lily, as it were, and your handsomest potted plants will both thrive and be seen to their best advantage in tank terrariums, spread with several inches of coarse, clean, white pebbles. Technique as follows: submerge the entire pot in water. Soak and drain it before placing it in the tank. Space your plants so that the leaves won't touch, and fill in the scene with unusually shaped rocks, or with sprawling vines such as Zebrina and Kenilworth ivy, growing from smaller pots. Zebrina cuttings will root quickly in water glasses concealed behind large flower pots. As to grass: it's attractive, but it just may go rank on you, and require trimming and occasional reseeding. Don't overestimate your own capacity for vigilance. If you skip the grass, sprinkle the gravel and cover the terrarium, you can reduce maintenance to occasional waterings.

7.

THE TERRARIUM AS NURSERY:

Growing from Seed, Cuttings

and Bulbs

Growing your own plants from seed, cuttings and bulbs is an indoor gardening adventure in itself, whose ramifications, advantages and techniques are the substance of the chapter. Heading the list is the obvious merit of assuring yourself a reserve supply of glass gardening material. You can also grow your own houseplants, and get annuals and vegetables off to an early start. This is really the most scientific section of our entire treatise: if you jot down planting and germination data, you'll go from strength to strength.

TERRARIUM PLANTS FROM SEED

Use sterile milled sphagnum for starting all kinds of seed. (If you plant directly in the terrarium, spread ½ inch of drainage gravel over the bottom before pouring in the sphagnum soil.) It takes 4 cups of this milled moss to fill a single fiber jiffy flat measuring 7½ inches long by 5½ inches wide by 2¼ inches deep. Measure the moss into a plastic bag, add 1½ cups of water, and knead the bag until all of the water has been absorbed. Then pour the moist mixture into the flat, leveling the surface and corners evenly with a block of wood.

The larger the nursery terrarium, the easier it is to plant and care for. The little commercial seed-starting greenhouses of glass or plastic will do splendidly, but you can make an excellent nursery of any tank terrarium that's easy to cover. The same is true of jiffy flats and planting trays, which can be lidded with plastic. But for extremely fine seed and slow-growing plants, I prefer the smaller plastic boxes

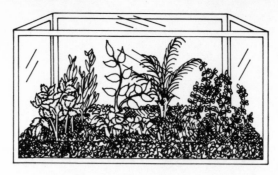

and containers that are used for storing and refrigerating food.

The electric soil heating cable (see Sources of Supply) now enables you to start seeds anywhere, and to step up the germination time of even the most difficult seeds with cable-supplied bottom heat. Although I usually start my seeds on a shelf over a floor heating outlet, the cable has rendered such make-do's obsolete. The 120-volt cables can be plugged into ordinary electrical outlets. They come in different sizes, ranging from a 3-foot length, which heats 1.5 square feet, to a 6-foot cable that heats 3 square feet. They are waterproofed with a sturdy plastic coat, and you may use them with complete safety in moist soil or even in water.

A 3-foot cable has the capacity to heat a several-gallon terrarium, or 6 jiffy flats under plastic. (Jiffy flats are made of peatmoss, pressed into a fibrous substance.) You can insulate by spreading masonite or several layers of cardboard (to which the cable can be taped) lengthwise under the planter. Such insulating helps to direct the heat upwards, and to maintain an even germinating soil temperature of from 70° to 75°. Most seeds will germinate satisfactorily at this heat; some of the fussier plants, particularly tropical ones, may require 75° plus.

If you are experimentally minded, you'll want to have a soil thermometer (see Sources of Supply) so that you can test the soil temperature and make note of what works best with which plants.

Watering of seedlings in covered containers will be more frequent than in permanent container gardens, although such seedlings are less demanding than they would be elsewhere. If you must water, use the oft-recommended "mist-ifier" or rubber hand-sprinkler. The seedling terrarium will also require *more ventilation* so as to harden the plants and to prevent excessive dampness.

Transplanting will frequently be in order, and seedlings removed from crowded flats to individual fiber pots won't suffer setbacks when they're moved outdoors. Use a kitchen fork for transplanting chores; the separated tines lessen the possibility of severing tender roots or of damaging neighboring plants.

As foretold above, growing from seed can equip you to be your own self-supplier of the most useful small plants for filling glass gardens, thereby eliminating much time-consuming searching and shopping. A skeleton list follows:

WOODLAND PLANTS

Most autumn-ripening seeds remain dormant until spring. Simply scatter them, or cover them lightly, as outdoors they grow on nothing more than mere contact with the moist ground .Conifer seeds, after a ripening period of stratification, should be started in a well-drained composition of milled peat, sand, and woodland humus. (Note: Stratification is the process whereby seed is layered in a slightly moist mixture of sand combined with shredded *and* milled sphagnum, which will supply both oxygen and moisture. This procedure duplicates the natural process by which seeds are buried under snow-packed leaves. Besides protecting the seed, stratification helps to mature the embryo and to soften hard seed-coverings. Refrigeration has simplified the now-antiquated practice of burying wooden boxes of layered seed in the ground. More about stratification later on.)

FOLIAGE PLANTS

Grow these low-light-intensity plants as terrarium subjects, potting them for individual window display when they outgrow their miniature landscape environs. Quick-growing *Coffea arabica* has shining oval leaves. The mature tree bears starry white flowers as well as the red berries from which the popular beverage is made. *Palm seed,* hard and nutlike, given warmth and terrarium moisture, will germinate in 6 months to a year. Other easily grown foliage plants are: umbrella palm (*Cyperus alternifolius*), rubber plant (*Ficus elastica*), Australian silk oak (*Grevillea*), ornamental banana (*Musa*), *Schefflera,* philodendron, and *Peperomia*.

Another category of tiny foliage trees growable from seed is the citrus family. Using ripe seeds, you can raise lemon, orange and grapefruit seedling plants.

HOUSEPLANTS FROM SEED

Yes, you can buy them, but it's far more rewarding to start from

CITRUS TREE
FROM SEEDS

African violet blossoming in a brandy bowl.

scratch and watch the ever-miraculous evolution of seed to flower. Besides, you'll be able to obtain varieties not available through general sources.

African Violets

Generally, seed-grown African violets flower within 6 to 9 months. An exception is the early-blooming 'True Blue', which blossoms in 5 months.

Specialty nurserymen offer such a generous selection of seed that hand-pollination and seed-saving are unnecessary. You can buy single and double-flowered varieties in homogeneous packets or in colorful mixtures. Any of the packaged African violet soils comprised of sand, sphagnum and humus will do, but sterile horticultural sphagnum is unfailingly dependable. Scatter the seed, and firm it on the moistened moss with a small block of wood. Cover the container and put it in a sunny window. Given an even 75° temperature, the seeds should germinate within 20 days. The first grasslike spears are insignificant, but then come the more convincing cotyledons, or seed leaves; after they unfold, they're followed by leaves bearing unmistakable African violet characteristics. After germination, move the seed box out of the sun, but take care that it still receives abundant light.

Some 6 weeks after sprouting, when a seedling has produced 2 or more dime-sized leaves, transplant it. Crowded seedlings develop into scrawny, inferior plants, so give them plenty of space for sprawling. Two-inch clay pots will supply enough room for this first transplanting, and as the plants continue to grow, move them into larger pots. Cover individual transplants with inverted water glasses, or move them into larger nursery terrariums. African violet seedlings can tolerate more warmth than older plants, so try to maintain a daytime temperature in the vicinity of 80° with a nocturnal drop of 10° or so. Give the transplants the full benefit of *sunless light,* and don't expose them even to weak sunlight until after several months of leaf growth.

Cacti and Succulents

If given steady 60° warmth, the seeds of many of these plants will germinate within two weeks—but don't expect flowers for a year or more, the exact time being dependent on the variety. Sow the seeds in porous, sandy soil, and remove the cover at the first sign of growth; standard cacti-succulent caution: moisture may cause rot. Do not expose the seedling to direct sunlight, and when the plants develop spines, transplant them to individual or community pots.

Cacti-succulents grow uncovered in an 8" high bowl. Included are a 4½" beavertail cactus, a 5" succulent, and a 1½" barrel cactus.

Fibrous Begonias

Dustlike begonia seed will vanish into the air if you so much as sneeze. Pour this fine seed into a creased sheet of paper and trickle it onto the moist sphagnum. With ample light at room temperature, the tiny rounded cotyledons will make their nursery-box debut within weeks or a very few months; precise time-span varies with species. When the seedlings come to touch each other, it's time to transplant. If the leaves turn yellow, you'll know that nourishment is in order: give them bi-monthly feedings of soluble plant food. As growth demands, shift them to larger pots, shielding them at all times from hot sun.

Gloxinias

You may sow single strains or, if you like surprises, try planting a mixture. Other things being equal, you'll have flowers in 6 to 9 months. Try not to bunch the seeds; distribute them as generally as possible. A germination period of 1 to 2 weeks is customary, assuming covered seed boxes exposed to a well-lighted window at a temperature range of 65° to 70°. When the plants have produced 4 leaves, move them to 2½-inch jiffy pots of *un*milled (shredded) sphagnum, and transfer the pots to a larger covered container. Increase ventilation by gradually raising the lid, removing it entirely in several weeks' time. Feed the plants regularly with soluble food, and shift them to permanent 4-inch to 6-inch clay pots when the roots show through the sides of the fiber pots. If the plants are spindly, strengthen them by burying the two bottommost leaves and covering the stem with soil up to the next set of leaves.

Double Gloxinias. You can buy seed that will grow into giant double-flowering gloxinias, about 75% of which will produce the double flowers, the remainder emerging as huge single blossoms, in the same colors as their twinned relatives.

Ferns

Ferns, it so happens, are produced from spores and not from seed. These specklike organisms cling to the back of the pinnules or sometimes to the entire frond. Collecting your own spores can be tricky: green seed, left too long, will shrivel up and then shed, leaving only a dry brown covering which is all too easily mistaken for the absent spores. With a strong magnifying glass you can differentiate between true spores and seed coverings.

But if you buy seed that's been collected and prepared by experts (see Sources of Supply), you'll be assured of material that's in top growing condition. Maidenhair, ocean spray, Boston fern, bird's nest and sword fern are only a few of the tropical and native ferns listed in specialty nursery catalogues. These, and others, are also available in mixed packets.

Fern seed is grown in sterilized milled sphagnum (and after you go through the ordeal of distributing the seed over the surface, you'll know why medieval Europeans were convinced that the dustlike fern spores could make you invisible).

Moist sunless humidity is crucial. If the sphagnum dries out, mist it with rainwater (I can dream, can't I?) or with *tapwater that's been sterilized by boiling.* As you'd expect, tropical varieties can stand more heat than can native ferns, but a temperature of 65° is acceptable to one and all. Don't expect ferns to pop up overnight; germination takes 20 days to a month and longer. The first manifestations are a microscopic, moldlike green growth called *Prothallia.* Sex organs develop immediately on the undersides, and fertilization takes place prior to the appearance of the first tiny fronds, which can take as long as several months. When the seedlings are 1 inch tall, transplant them to another larger covered container, or invert water glasses over individual clay pots. You may elect to start your ferns in a *fernarium,* comprising a handy ready-made fern-starting kit containing sterilized planting media, a covered plastic container, and a generous supply of spores (see Sources of Supply). If you follow the accompanying directions to the letter, you're virtually assured of complete success.

Orchids

Growing orchids from seed was once the province of the botanical laboratory, so technical a project was it considered. Now, courtesy an *orchid seed starter kit* (see Sources of Supply), you can grow these exotic plants at home. Each kit contains germinating flasks, agar jelly (in which seeds are sown), filter papers, a wire seed-planting loop, and a bottle of calcium hypochlorite granules for disinfecting seed. Orchids are prolific producers, but few of the many thousands of seeds packed in each pod will develop without agar (a gelatin-like seaweed by-product), and nutrients which compensate for the absence of a natural fungus needed to stimulate the embryos.

Follow instructions carefully; sterilize the agar jelly and the flasks in a pressure cooker, as well as the seed itself, with the enclosed disinfectant. The flasks may be set upright or horizontally; the agar will solidify on the bottom. Then distribute the wet seed over the jelly by means of the planting wire, and plug the flask with cotton. With filtered light and warm temperature (between 68° and 86°), germination will occur in 4 to 6 weeks. When the third leaf appears, a seedling is ready to be transplanted. Again, this could be a matter of months to a year, depending on the genus and on the rapidity of development.

Some seedlings will be well-rooted; others, barely visible. These latter must be helped along with more shade and humidity. You transplant as follows: lift the seedlings from the flask with a notched flat stick; wash off the agar in warm water; then plant them in community pots of Osmunda or pulverized bark. House the potted tender seedlings in well-ventilated nursery terrariums, where the growing medium is neither too wet nor too dry.

TENDER FLOWERING ANNUALS AND VEGETABLES

Get your flowering annuals off to an early start by sowing their seeds in terrarium greenhouses. I sow seeds in small fiber flats that are set right in the terrarium on a bottom cover of moist pebbles. One 7½-inch by 5½-inch jiffy flat will comfortably accommodate 100 large seeds, 200 small ones, or about 300 extremely fine seeds.

Make a shallow furrow with a pencil, and sow the seed evenly in it. Cover larger seeds twice the depth of their diameter. (*Note:* Fine seed is never covered; it is scattered on the surface of moist, firmly packed moss.) Moist seed flats that are glass-covered needn't be watered at all until after germination, which for most annuals will be after approximately 2 weeks. As soon as the seedlings begin to sprout, *remove the glass during the day;* if you don't ventilate, the stems will become leggy. Retain the needed warmth by replacing the glass again at night.

Again the familiar but all-important refrain: uncovered nurseries will require more water. Use a rubber hand-sprinkler whenever the moss, dark black when moist, turns brown.

Seedlings need all the light you can give them. Evenly distributed overhead light is best. The plantings will instinctively turn (tropism, you recall) toward the window, so rotate the flats frequently.

As soon as seedlings produce 4 leaves, they need elbow room. Put them in fiber pots, packing the roots firmly in shredded sphagnum. You'll have to add weekly applications of a soluble fertilizer, because sphagnum is low in nutrients. Store your transplants in a plastic tray or, if you've got room, in a well-ventilated terrarium, giving them plenty of sunlight until it's time to transfer them to the garden. Watch, meanwhile, for signs of damping off or rot—the inevitable result of too much moisture: it's better to maintain seedlings on the dry side by using ample ventilation.

Vegetables

Tender annual vegetables such as peppers, tomatoes, and eggplant can be started from seed, as can hardier broccoli, cabbage, and cauliflower. Germinating time for melons, squash and other tender annual vine crops can be shortened considerably by starting the seeds in glass-covered fiber pots. I find that the normal germination period of 10 to 14 days can be reduced to 5. Moist humidity coupled with inadequate light can make these seedlings all stems, so remove the cover as soon as they sprout, and give the plants plenty of evenly distributed light.

Time the planting of your annuals, be they floral or vegetable, according to the final frost dates in your growing area; seed started 6 to 8 weeks in advance of this date will be sturdily ready for outdoor life by the time the nights are frost-free.

SEED STORAGE AND TESTING

Stratification

This process was briefly defined in the earlier section of this chapter, with reference to conifers, under "Woodland Plants." Stratification is actually a method of storing seed that ripens too late in the season to start its growth cycle. For this purpose, use a fruit jar. Spread a layer of moist stratifying medium (sand plus both shredded *and* milled sphagnum) over the bottom of the jar, and on it place the seeds; then, another layer of the moist medium, and so on—seeds, medium, seeds, in layers until the jar is filled. If the seed you're using is particularly fine, layer it in strips of plastic so that you won't lose it 'mongst the moss. Most autumn-ripened seed requires 3 months of cold storage, but nuts, for example, take from early autumn right through spring.

Seeds other than nuts that require stratification include conifers and stone fruits, apple, pear, tulip tree, elm, sycamore, *Franklinia,* viburnum, redbud, roses and Ginkgo.

Refrigerate your covered seed jars, or store them anywhere in the dark where the temperature is above freezing but below the 50° sprouting line. Check unrefrigerated seed from time to time; it might germinate. If it does, plant the sprouts indoors temporarily. Normally, stratified seed is sown out of doors, in a cool, shaded coldframe or nursery row, after the weather has warmed up.

Seed Testing

It's important to test the viability of homegrown seed and the contents of leftover seed packets; it'll save time and disappointment at planting time—and the glass garden is the place to do it. Use moist shredded sphagnum moss in just about any container: it can be as workaday as a glass tumbler upended over saucer of moss. My own favorite seed-tester, ideal for the purpose, is an old plastic fishing-tackle box sectioned into individual compartments.

If you sprinkle about 25 seeds of a kind, you can estimate the approximate percentage of germination likelihood: 80%, for example, if 20 seeds germinate. Some seed will sprout almost instantly; others will take several days; older seed will take longer. Any seed will germinate (if ever it's going to) in average room temperature; I put my tackle box on top of a shelf above a floor register, but a sunny window will do nicely, provided that you cover the container with a dark cloth. Make certain that you label carefully each kind of seed that you test.

Storing

After you've completed your tests, store the sealed airtight jars on a cool dry shelf. During humid summer months, a small package of silica gel or dried shredded sphagnum will absorb any humidity-induced excess moisture inside the jars.

Some seed, such as sweet corn, can be kept for 2 years. Other kinds—squash, lettuce, cucumber, turnip, spinach and watermelon—will remain viable for as long as 5 years.

ROOTING PLANTS FROM CUTTINGS

SOFTWOOD CUTTINGS

Among the many hardy perennials that can be perpetuated and increased by soft, or greenwood, cuttings are *Dianthus,* chrysanthemums, candytuft (*Iberis*), and rock cress (*Arabis*). The best length for such cuttings is from 3 to 6 inches; larger lengths will produce spindly plants. With few exceptions, *cut at the base of a joint.* When you can't obtain a heel (that is, piece of bark from the main stem), select a vigorous terminal or lateral shoot as your source.

Clean sand is the safest rooting medium, as soil contains vegetable

Rooting leaf and stem cuttings in sand.

matter that could cause damping off. Spread the sand 3 inches deep on the bottom of the terrarium, and moisten it well. A weak vinegar solution (¼ teaspoon to 1 quart of water) will supply the acidity needed for proper rooting. Remove most of the leaves from the cuttings. Pack the ends firmly in the sand about an inch deep. Allow 2 inches between cuttings; water lightly, and seal the cover, providing ample shade for the first 10 days. Then elevate the glass, but continue shading the plants until you see evidence of growth. After the root systems are firmly established, remove the glass entirely. Add water whenever the sand gets dry. Watch vigilantly for damping off and remove infected cuttings immediately.

Once your plants are rooted, transplant them to sifted garden soil and leaf mold, maintaining shade for several days until they become acclimated to the sun. Don't reuse the same sand for another batch of cuttings.

Pachysandra

This useful ground cover, a softwood cutting special, will grow in moist shade anywhere. The average gardener can't have too much of it. The plants are expensive to buy, an excellent reason for rooting them from cuttings; they'll start either in water or in moist sand flats. I tend to forget to water my own cuttings until they've almost dried up—and so I lost most of them until I started rooting them in covered glass containers. Now I stick the cuttings in moist sand, cover them, forget them, and still keep my plants.

HARDWOOD CUTTINGS

This is a slow procedure. The cuttings are taken from dormant shrubs, and it takes the entire winter for rooting callouses to form. Cut 8-inch lengths from strong year-old wood; tie them in bundles, bury them in moist sphagnum in a covered terrarium, and go about your business.

Dim light and 40° temperature are the conditions conducive to the formation of callouses on the butt ends. Roots will form from these callouses, come spring, and you can then plant them outside in the moist shade.

Grafting Scions

Few gardeners graft their own trees today, but covered glass containers provide moist storage conditions for the winter housing of woody deciduous twigs intended for grafting. In late autumn, after the leaves have fallen, one cuts vigorous 12-inch shoots, from the growth of the season just past. The shoots are tied into bundles, packed in moist sphagnum in the manner of hardwood cuttings, and stored in a cool dark place.

IMPROVISED GREENHOUSES FOR CUTTINGS

The Plastic Bag

These are instantaneous, cheap, and available. You can make it into a greenhouse to root your cuttings in minutes. Take a sturdy one, and pour a mixture of sand and milled sphagnum into the bottom. Moisten this mix well, insert your cuttings, snap an elastic band around the top of the bag, and place it in the light. Water only if conditions so warrant.

Fruit Jars

Eureka: another homely source of greenhouse supply. You can increase your stock of roses and other shrubs in the following simple fashion: take 4-inch cuttings from summer greenwood or hardwood slips; stick them in the ground or in a container of moist sand, and invert fruit jars over them. Keep them in a cool shade until the new roots form. *Fait accompli!*

All rooting in a shallow pan of sand.
a. leaf cutting.
b. Mason jar covering "mum" cutting.
c. English ivy stem cutting.

ROOTING THE SHOOTS

RUNNERS, OFFSETS AND SUCKERS

Plant shoots are easy to propagate. Pot up runners near the parent plant in a 3″ pot filled with suitable soil (see Plant Encyclopedia). Secure the shoots to the soil with a hairpin. When roots form, sever from parent plant. Or you can cut away the runner to begin with, and use it as a terrarium subject, potted up as for a cutting. Either way, it should have shade and humidity until roots form. Boston fern and chlorophytum are often propagated this way.

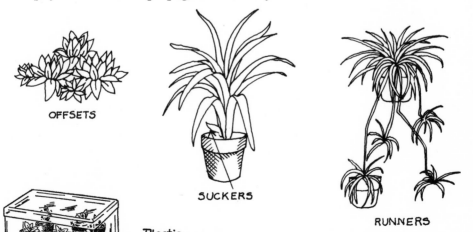

OFFSETS

SUCKERS

RUNNERS

Plastic refrigerator box for small pots.

Offsets are short-stemmed shoots or rosettes formed at base of plant. They can be pulled off the parent and potted for a quick source of new plants. Dendrobium (orchid) and succulents such as sempervivum can be increased this way.

Suckers are secondary shoots which start from an underground root. Pot them in suitable soil and keep moist. Scoop them out with some of the underground roots from the parent plant still attached, and put into terrarium or set into small pot.

AIR LAYERING TIPS

When large growing plants like crotons, philodendrons, and dracaenas get leggy, you can propagate them by rooting the top shoots or tips. Cut halfway through the stems, on a slant, just below the top leaves. Wrap dampened sphagnum moss around and in the wound. (a) Tie loosely with cord. Cover with plastic (b). Keep moss wet at all times. To lessen evaporation, set plant in large plastic sheet tied at top (c). Keep shaded. Several weeks later, when moss AIR-LAYERING is filled with roots, sever tip from the parent stem and use it as a terrarium subject (for very large tanks), or as a potted plant (d).

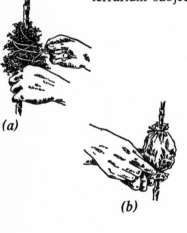

(a)

(b)

(c)

(d)

ROOTING SPRING FLOWERING BULBS

It's much easier to root a pot of these bulbs for indoor forcing in a terrarium than it is to bury them out of doors in a coldframe. Here's my procedure: I take several of my largest terrarium tanks, and spread an inch of coarse gravel over the bottoms. I then fill them with as many bulb pots as they'll hold. To conserve space and to utilize the height of the terrarium as well as its other dimensions, I stack the pots by inverting empty clay flower pots over the bottom row, so as to avoid injuring the sprouts with the pot above. Then I lightly moisten each pot, and cover the terrarium with window glass, leaving a half-inch margin at either end. I find that not much watering is needed, but it's advisable to check the bulbs now and then for signs of molding. I then place these rooting terrariums in a dim corner of my basement, where the temperature hovers consistently around 50°. Almost any similar location above freezing will do, if it's sufficiently dark so as not to encourage premature sprouting.

Sound root systems are essential to sturdy stems, healthy foliage, and flowers. Rooting time varies with species: French-Roman hyacinths, crocuses of the Vanguard and the Sieberi species, and miniature rockery *Iris Reticulata,* potted in unenriched, well-drained garden soil in mid-October, will root in about 5 weeks and be ready for Christmas bloom. However, most of the other bulbs such as hybrid hyacinths, tulips, narcissus, grape hyacinth (*Muscari*), and the later-blooming, large-flowered crocuses will require a 3-month rooting period. Indications of proper rooting are plump, impatient yellow sprouts, or actual roots appearing through drainage holes of pots.

Once the plants have rooted, move the pots into the light, gradually introducing them to a cool but sunny window. (You'll note a uniformity about this entire transplant-and-induction-to-light procedure.) The little early-flowering crocuses and iris that bloom on the fringe of winter's retreating snow do best for me on a cool bright basement window. If you've no place to go other than a hot dry room, retain the essential moisture by inverting water glasses over the sprouts.

EATING OUT OF GLASS CONTAINERS

MUSHROOMS

Growing mushrooms in one's own basement has become a popular pastime, although the modern basement is too often a utility room, and the cool moist growing conditions favored by *Agaricus* are more likely to be found in the old-fashioned cellar, damp and dark. Our solution is, of course, the terrarium, where you can grow your own mushrooms no matter what kind of basement, if any, you've got.

You can set preplanted trays inside the terrarium, or spread the spawn on a layer of moist compost topped by an inch of humus. A dollar's worth of mushroom spawn will cover 10 to 12 feet, and provide you with several plantings. Soil must be moist, but never wet; 55° to 65° is the ideal temperature; light *per se* won't impede mushroom growth, but direct sun must be avoided. If you sow too thickly, your mushrooms will come up small.

About 3 weeks after planting, tiny, buttonlike mushroom caps will rear their heads. Mushrooms tend to grow in "flushes"; i.e., batches of them come up simultaneously. Pick them when the veil that connects the lower part of the cap with the stem breaks, and the cap becomes flat. After you've cut one "flush," an apparently dormant period may ensue for some days; then, another flush presents itself. If your growing conditions are good, a crop will produce for several months. When food in the humus is exhausted, production will taper off to a few stray buttons. Time to start anew: scrape off the top layer, add fresh soil, and plant crops right up to the onset of warm weather.

The preplanted trays I referred to earlier come as part of handy mushroom gardens, obtainable through several growers from October through April; the *preplanted mushroom planter* comes complete with soil, spawn, and a plastic-covered planting tray. (See Sources of Supply.)

ONION SPROUTS

It may surprise you that *Allium cepa* is, in fact, a lily! Well, for its notoriously unfloral fragrance it more than compensates with its flavor. Liven up your winter salads with small leftover onions in the bottom of the vegetable bin. Set the bulbs, bottoms down, on moist moss in any large covered container. Sprouts will grow long, thick and tasty, their color varying from yellow to bright green depending on the amount of light in their vicinity.

SPICY CRESS

Another tangy salad ingredient, supplied for and by yourself with the aid of a 12-inch by 24-inch terrarium containing several shallow plastic planting trays filled with moist moss, shredded sphagnum or potting soil. Cress does require some fertilizer containing nitrogen. Scatter the seed thickly, cover the container, and cut the plants when they measure about 2 inches. Use scissors for snipping. After several such harvestings, pull out the roots and plant another crop. Start seed at 7-day intervals, feast on cress all winter long, and toss out your vitamin pills.

TERRARIUMS FOR STORAGE

RESERVE PLANT MATERIAL

We started this chapter by citing the advantages of a reserve supply of materials. Every glass gardener will want to maintain a surplus of mosses, ferns and plants for planting and replacing—and the place to do it is right inside a terrarium. The storage terrarium is planted, not to show, but to grow. I maintain two gardens in glass for plants-in-waiting; one, for tropicals, is indoors; the other, for hardy woodland plants, resides in the woodshed, where condensing moisture frequently freezes in attractive frost patterns without injury to the hardy occupants. During extremely cold weather, I introduce these frozen plants to indoor warmth, using the basement as an intervening stage. Both indoor and outdoor storage gardens are covered with plastic; they receive plenty of light, and need little care.

SOIL MIXTURES FOR SOWING AND POTTING

Simplify future potting activities for whatever purpose by mixing several of the soil formulae you use most frequently and storing them in empty tank terrariums. I find that if soils are dampened lightly and covered, they keep moist enough to be used instantly for either seed-sowing or potting. *Be certain to label these soil mixtures* for ready identification.

8.

DRIED ARRANGEMENTS

UNDER GLASS

Dried arrangements are exceedingly popular as part of permanent home decor; you can attain the colors and effect you want for any part of the house without worrying about replacements. And, under glass, dried arrangements take on a fresh, lifelike luminosity.

They do, of course, limit your choice of container: the stalks of dried plants aren't pliant, so you'll have to use something with at least a fist-sized opening. This still affords you ample latitude: brandy snifters, keepsake domes, yesterday's cloches (reproduced today in glass and plastic), old-fashioned candy jars, glass teapots and sugar bowls, and assorted miscellany.

SUGGESTED MATERIALS AND WHERE TO FIND THEM

Some showy native grasses can be found in orchards and barnyards. Others, such as foxtail, redtop and Timothy, reside in meadows, as do goldenrod, yarrow, milkweed pods and pearly everlastings (*Anaphalis margaritacea*), all excellent candidates. Dock (*Rumex*) grows in moist waste places; cattails, bur reed (*Sparganium*), and Joe-Pye weed (*Eupatorium purpureum*) live in swampy ground; salt marshes is where you'll find mallows and seaside lavender (*Limonium carolinianum*). Ferns, as versatile when dried as fresh, grow, as usual, in shaded moist woods.

The garden yield includes: baby's breath, silvery-grey Artemisias, and any dried seedheads, pods and husks that catch your eye. Miniature annuals such as dwarf marigolds and zinnias are delightful in smaller containers. Other fine garden possibilities are pussy willow, daffodils and violas.

112

And also grass, which isn't always greener in the other fellow's yard! In even a short garden row, you can grow an abundance of reliable ornamental grasses, as follows: quaking grass (*Briza maxima*), Job's tears (*Coix lachryma*), foxtail millet (*Setaria italica*), hare's-tail grass (*Lagarus ovatus*) and animated oats (*Avena sterilis*). Easy-to-grow everlastings include statice (*Sinuata*), globe amaranth (Gomphrena), money plant (*Lunaria*), immortelle (*Xeranthemum*), strawflower (*Helichrysum*), Bells of Ireland (*Molucella laevis*), and the ruby-seeded jewels-of-Opar (*Talinum paniculatum*).

Also in the backyard grow such berried plants as: rose haws, holly, bittersweet (*Celastrus scandens*), beauty-berry (*Callicarpa*) and pyracantha. Rose haws keep well, but turn brownish with age. All dried berries will shrink to some extent, but fleshy pyracantha in particular should be used only in containers that will permit you to replace them occasionally with fresh berries.

Don't overlook trees. Ash, tulip and locust have artistic seed pods. Avoid needled conifer foliage that will shed. I use only cedar and arborvitae; cedar, especially, dries into an appealing blue-grey shade.

GROWING MATERIAL FOR DRIED ARRANGEMENTS FROM SEED

The staples of bottled bouquets are ornamental grasses and everlastings.

Several short garden rows will yield enough dried material to fill dozens of containers. Choose a sunny, well-drained location where the soil is moderately rich. Sow the larger seeds well under the surface as usual; scatter the fine seed on the surface. Sow evenly and thinly, allowing 18 to 24 inches between rows.

Plant most varieties when the days are warm and the nights frost-free. The instructions printed on each seed packet will indicate which varieties require early planting. Strawflowers germinate best in cool and constantly moist soil.

These plantings will require cultivation—to keep down weeds, aerate roots, and to conserve soil moisture during dry weather. It's a confusing task to weed rows of ornamental grasses when weed grass is also present; better, if in doubt, to let both grow unimpeded until harvest, rather than risk uprooting the desirable species.

Plants thinned so as to stand 12 inches apart will grow bushy and produce more heavily. Feed them only with balanced plant food, as directed. Too much nitrogen will make them too leafy at the expense of the flowers and seed heads.

WHEN TO HARVEST AND HOW TO DRY

Gather your material on a clear and sunny day, preferably at high noon when the plants are dry. Use scissors for ferns and grasses; pruning shears for stouter stems. You'll want short stems for bottled bouquets, but it's always wise to leave them a little longer than your estimated need.

Grasses ripen at different times between early summer and the first frost. Cut grass after it has flowered, but before its seed is fully developed. If you cut at varying stages of the grass's growth, you'll come up with some lovely gradations of color, ranging from soft springtime pastels through opulent summer greens to the warm mellow tones of autumn.

OTHER GLEANING TIPS

Pick:

Milkweed, when its pods have fully formed.

Cattails, in June, when spikes are still small and firm.

Joe-Pye weed, when the buds begin to open, so as to preserve the magenta coloring.

Goldenrod, when the florets are fully out; you'll retain the glowing color.

Dock, when the seed has just formed and again when it's fully ripe; the two cuttings will provide you with both green and brown seed stalks.

Strawflowers and other everlastings, before the flower buds open; otherwise the centers will turn brown.

Pussy willows, in the early spring, when the catkins are plump but before the golden pollen-laden staminate blossoms open fully. Dry out the wood by placing the cuttings in a waterless vase.

DRYING

You can dry plants quickly wherever there is no dampness and the light is subdued. Use an attic, a utility room, or an airy closet. Flowers will mold if it's damp, and if placed in too bright an exposure, they'll lose some of their natural coloring.

Here's the general technique: tie a dozen plants or so into a small bundle, and snap an elastic band tightly around the stem ends. (They'll shrink as they dehydrate, but the trusty rubber band will contract correspondingly. Then, suspend the bunches from a clothes-line, spaced so that they won't touch; save space by tying several smaller bundles to a single coat hanger. Now, wait. Allow at least ten days for drying. When your material is dry, pack it, one layer deep, in shallow but ample-sized cardboard boxes, or let it hang until you're ready to start the arranging.

Daffodils, violas and summer annuals such as zinnias and mari-golds are dried head down in a box full of ordinary borax or of any commercial drying preparation that contains *silica gel.* (See Sources of Supply.) Flowers dried with borax will take two weeks in the process; silica gel cuts the drying time down to seven days.

TOOLS, MATERIALS AND HOW TO DO IT

Besides your chief ingredients, which are the plants themselves, you will want: *For planting,* floral clay, aquarium gravel, dried moss strips or lichen, needle-point holders, rubber cement. *For assembling,* a wooden dowel, a tablespoon, scissors, kitchen tongs (or tweezers for small-scale stuff), and a length of wire. If your chosen container has no cover, you'll have to provide one.

To prepare the base, spread floral clay generously over the bottom of the glass to a depth of about 1 inch. This is done by dropping lumps of clay into the container and spreading it into a central mold with the dowel. I like this clay base myself, but it's also possible to use a needled flower holder: insert it with the above-mentioned kitchen tongs. But you'll have to anchor the holder to the glass with a coil of clay which you firm over both the floor of the container and the bottom of the holder, then joining the twain with dowel. Make sure that both glass and holder are completely dry for this operation; otherwise, the clay won't stick.

Now to arrange the bouquet inside the container. If the mere thought frightens you, I suggest you practice with a few grasses until you get the hang of it. Suggestion: make perforations in the clay with a wire before you try to anchor the stems of fragile fern fronds and grasses; it'll save you lots of stem breakage and several tantrums. Also, place taller material around the outside of the glass where it can serve as a kind of measuring rod and eliminate considerable guesswork.

Follow the usual design guidelines. A special design hazard to keep in mind, however, is berry shrinkage: allow for this by putting in solid clumps of neighboring material. Dock and artemista serve as good filler, as do grasses. Finally, finish the arrangement by camouflaging the base under dried moss strips, bits of lichen-covered bark, or aquarium gravel, white or colored. Spread this last-named base-concealer about with a tablespoon.

Seal the container tightly by spreading rubber cement on the rim, as well as on the inside of the cover. Check both container and contents thoroughly before sealing: *everything's got to be completely dry, or the arrangement will decay.* A tightly sealed dry arrangement should last for years without losing much of its original color unless it's exposed to direct sunlight. Some fading is inevitable; white flowers, for example, become creamy with age, as does white everything else. But it's a gradual mellowing process.

At the earliest indication of humidity, remove the cover and place the container in a warm dry place. You can forestall the accumulation of humidity during a prolonged period of storage by placing a concealed spoonful of silica gel around the base when you create the arrangement.

Come spring and the first bowlful of daffodils, and you can relegate your bottled bouquets to storage, in a dim, dry place, until next October. At which time you'll be very happy to see them, either as they are, or refurbished with some additional flowers.

CONTAINERS AND CONTENTS: SUGGESTIONS FOR DRIED ARRANGEMENTS

1. *Brandy glass:* a snifter of autumn. Job's tears, rye, assorted grasses, dock and Artemisia complement a central cluster of strawflowers and bittersweet.

2. *Apothecary jar:* a cylinder of predominantly purple. Globe amaranth, jewels-of-Opar, quaking grass and a fern frond or two.

3. *Candy jar:* Surround an antique figurine with royal fern pinnules, a plume of foxtail, quaking grass, and globe amaranth rosettes tightly clustered in the foreground.

4. *Bubble bowl:* effective simplicity. A few tropical wood roses, arranged with your own dried ferns and grasses.

5. *Spring promise:* April recaptured. Fill your favorite container with pussy willow, trumpet daffodils and violas.

6. *Cloches and Keepsake Domes.* Everything here works just as it does for other arrangements, except that these particular glass gardens are inverted *over* the bouquet, so that everything you plant in your floral clay base or needle-point holder, secured to a wooden base, must be trimmed to the size of the glass dome. Much less tricky. And therefore, you've got more latitude. Try a blue robin's egg as a foil

(Left) An apothecary jar with an opening 1¾ inches in diameter holds dry aquarium gravel about 2 inches deep. The trimmed dried plants (see 2 above) are inserted from back to foreground. Any tools mentioned for bottle plantings, page 53, can be used. (Right) The materials in the candy jar (see 3 above) are inserted by hand in the gravel flooring. Covers protect both dried arrangements from dust.

for delicately shaded golden grasses. Perpetuate the ephemeral loveliness of a swallowtail butterfly poised upon a cluster of everlastings. Combine cattails and marsh grasses with bits of driftwood, seashells, beach pebbles and waterworn glass. Create some sentimental souvenir arrangements, novel yet nostalgic, with ribbons, fans, Valentines, dance programs and other cherished memorabilia—not forgetting your family hero's war medals.

7. *Reliquaries.* A reverent Easter arrangement, created around a ceramic Madonna or similarly appropriate figurine, might include slivers from palm strips blessed in church on Palm Sunday, together with pussy willow, ferns, violas and other seasonal dried blossoms.

8. *The wedding bouquet.* Quick-drying silica gel preparations enable you to conserve these cherished corsages for ever and aye, almost. Proceed as follows: Separate the bouquet, discarding wilted flowers and preserving only unopened rosebuds and other blossoms still in good condition. Cut off the stems, and place the blossoms, heads up, in a tin cookie box in which you've spread several inches of silica gel. Space the flowers so that they don't touch, and cover them completely with a second layer of the silica gel compound. Now, cover the box and seal it with masking tape. After a week, take out the blossoms, and clean them with an artist's brush. Attach them to short lengths of wire wrapped with green floral tape, and arrange them as you like under a cloche, with ferns and (up to you!) bridegroom figurines.

9. *Bottle lamps.* I stated earlier in this chapter that a container for dried material should have a fist-sized opening. The bottle lamp, with its much narrower orifice, is clearly for the skilled and venturesome. If you're either or both, read on. First, you'll need an electric lamp adapter, and although these come in different sizes, I suggest that you not consider anything smaller than those for a gallon or, at the smallest, half-gallon bottle openings. Now: perform the clay base ceremony with your dowel, and make perforations in the clay, with a wire, for holding stems. Try to avoid the more brittle-stemmed drieds; create the bottle display from more pliable grasses, ferns, and smaller flowered everlastings. You'll drop in the grass stems first, and tilt the bottle so that the top of the grass rests on the glass; poke the stem into the perforated clay with a wire and, tilting and shaking, firm the clay around the base of each stem; camouflage the base with dry moss; make sure the bottle's dry, and insert the

adapter. In with the bulb; on with the shade and electricity. It's not easy, but you have a real conversation piece.

10. *Plastic holiday plaques.* Use a shallow plastic box, or an oval-shaped lid for which you construct a bottom, to feature the brightest berries from your winter garden. Mold clay to the bottom of the box, and insert short lengths of berried and evergreen twigs. Or trim a tiny evergreen tree with miniature ornaments, adding a seasonal angel. Soak the needled evergreens in any Christmas tree solution before you use them, or coat the needle-ends with glue. Place one—or a matching pair—in a window, on the mantel, or on the wall, using adhesive-backed picture hooks.

11. *Inside-outside window arrangement.* Use your inside window-panes and your storm windows as a double-faced glass garden. Fill up the intervening space with evergreens and dried materials, for a winter-long display that looks equally well from the outside in, or from the inside out. At holiday time, use bright berries or Christmas tree ornaments. Rose haws, especially those cut from wild shrubs, are effectively longlasting. Avoid hemlock and spruce, whose needles drop too quickly, in favor of pine, cedar, arborvitae and juniper, all longlived.

Once the storm window's in place, do all your arranging from the inside. Stick twig ends in small clay-filled pots or in detergent caps. Cold air and moisture will keep the greens and berries fresh until it's time to shift to screens. You'll add comfort as well as artistry with these inter-window displays, because the greenery acts as a buffer against draughts. It filters the sunlight for the benefit of your house-plants as well.

PICTURES UNDER GLASS WITH FERNS AND FLOWERS

This is an entirely separate and wonderfully effective variety of floral design under glass. An old-fashioned oval frame, sitting around unused, will gain a new lease on life as a setting for pressed viola faces. Small frames featuring individual fern fronds or sharply delineated leaves such as pin oak and sugar maple make attractive wall groupings.

To dry ferns and flowers for pressing, first lay them flat between several layers of newspaper; then add weights (dictionaries, old phone directories, bricks—anything that's ponderous). Each petal and pinnule must be pressed perfectly flat. Florets of such flowers as the delphinium may be pressed individually, then reassembled on the picture mat. Allow two weeks for complete drying. Small leaves, such as blueberry, sumac, chokeberry (*Aronia*), maple and sweet gum are pressed dry in the same way; you can retain autumn colors by sprinkling the leaves generously with borax.

Now for the assembling. Remove the back of the frame you've selected. Work on a background of heavy construction paper or fabric cut to size; you can use silk, velvet and other fabrics as coverings; another effective backdrop is embroidery wool wound around the construction paper. Arrange your pressed materials, designing as you would compose a painting, with both impact and harmony as your guiding principles. For depth and body, overlap the plant materials.

Once everything's in place, insert your floral picture into the frame; add screw eyes and wire, and it's ready for home display, gift-wrapping, or sale.

The Shadow Box

A variant on the floral picture is the shadow box, which allows you to create a three-dimensional arrangement of dried material that needn't be pressed, as the glass doesn't rest on the actual composition.

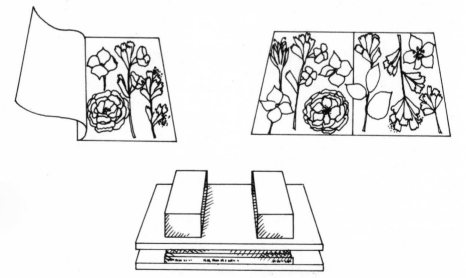

Plant materials can be press-dried between several sheets of newsprint or absorbent magazine pages weighted down with bricks, irons, etc. Change papers every few days or drying plants may mildew.

If you don't want to buy a shadow-box frame, simply take any old picture frame and cut glass to fit; then construct a box-frame approximately 1½ inches deep. Back it with a piece of plywood, which you can cover with felt or even with velvet. Then, *glue* on your selected dried materials, rather than merely place them, as you would for a shallow frame. The three-dimensional effect under glass is striking.

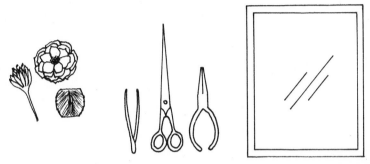

For the pressed flower picture in Color Plate V, you'll need dried plant materials, tweezers for handling delicate pieces, scissors for pruning and cutting (the vase shape was cut from a large leaf), and a picture frame with mat and glass to fit it. This mat was covered with vertical rows of embroidery wool wound all around it; velvet or other fabric are often used as a background too. The pliers are the very small ones used by milliners.

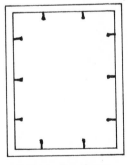

Lay the materials on the mat to make a pretty picture, overlapping for three-dimensional effect. Now carefully glue plants in place (use a transparent glue), or just put the glass over the mat, fit both into the frame, turn them over, and gently work upholstery tacks into the frame with pliers, to hold everything together. Kraft paper cut and glued to frame makes the final backing. Add screw eyes and wire, and your picture is ready for hanging.

9.
THE FESTIVE TERRARIUM

HOLIDAYS AND GIFTS

Commemorate Christmas and other holidays with gala arrangements in glass, and create some highly original, one-of-a-kind answers to the recurrent "What can I give them that they haven't already got?" problem.

When you present someone with any kind of glass garden, *always enclose printed instructions*. These should include identification of the plant material used, together with full information on the care and requirement of the garden—ventilation if it's needed, watering, temperature, light and heat. (See the Plant Encyclopedia for data.)

Some of the suggestions that follow make ideal gifts. Others, although you may bring yourself to part with them, will add immensely to holiday celebrations at home.

CHRISTMAS

Partridgeberries in Tree-Ornament Planters

A traditional part of New England giftgiving is the colorful partridge-berry bowl or sunshine jar, conveying Christmas in living color. It has retained its popularity over the years. In rural parts, partridge-berry was gathered in the upland woods before the snow, and all hands used to join in the planting around the kitchen table.

This festive favorite can be used to fill diminutive planters made from plastic Christmas tree ornaments—ball-shaped, bell-shaped or

122

octagonal. Remove the metal hangers and whatever toys or doodads are glued inside. If the ornament is made all in one piece, the top opening's usually large enough to permit your extracting the contents with a small tweezers. If it's made in two parts, reassemble it with rubber cement. Then proceed just as you would with miniature bottles (chapter 4), using your smallest planting tools. Poke the partridgeberry in, berry first. Use your smallest berries for this kind of planting, and whatever other short-stemmed plants you may have around.

Unless the original ornament hanger is very firmly glued, you'll be safer inserting a small, tightly-fitted cork reinforced with rubber cement. For hanging, thread an upholstery needle with colorful Christmas wrapping cord, poke it through the cork, and knot it in a loop. Done up in a small gala gift box, the finished plant-filled bauble makes a striking and novel little present.

Nativity Gardens

Strike a variant on the traditional crèches: glass containers are wonderfully appropriate settings for the traditional Nativity figures. Ferns, palms and small evergreens—i.e., a standard terrarium landscape—create an effective Holy Land backdrop—the palms being particularly appropriate to the semi-tropical region in which the first Christmas was celebrated. The plastic figures you've collected, constituting the colorful central action, won't be harmed by moisture. (No carved wooden treasures, please.) Depending on how large your glass proscenium is, you can include the entire Nativity cast; if you're restricted, just the Holy Family and an animal or two will be most effective. And, after the twelfth day of Christmas, remove the seasonal figures and enjoy your terrarium as usual.

Blooming Christmas Garden

Try forcing a few budded cherry tree twigs (see chapter 6). Forcing cherry boughs into flower to adorn the Christmas crèche is an old Central European custom, and recalls the "Cherry Tree Carol"— "when Joseph was a-walking." Cherry cuttings, actually, are believed by some historians to be the forerunner of the Christmas tree. They're called "Barbara boughs" because they are traditionally cut on December 4, the feast day of the (until recent decree) saint. And blossom bowls can conjure up, in glowing fashion, the delightful old legend about trees and flowers blooming in the snow on Christmas Eve.

Another authentic Christmas flower whose holiday associations may not be familiar to you is the violet, as is documented in the old Basque "Carol of the Flowers." They are further embroidered into the Christmas tapestry by the traditional belief that violets bloomed under the window of the Virgin Mary on the occasion of the Annunciation. So violets are entirely appropriate, forced into flower in a glass Nativity garden.

Christmas Bird Nest

The medieval imagination ran riot with floral and animal symbolism: it also envisioned birds nesting in the magical midnight hours of Christmas. Create a composition featuring a ceramic bird guarding a colorful clutch of miniature Christmas tree eggs in a planting of foliage.

Miniature Christmas Trees

Living trees. Plant a tiny live conifer (hemlock, spruce, pine or cedar) in a wide-mouthed glass container filled with soil and moss. Then trim the branches with tiny ornaments; water it, and cover the container.

A ceramic Santa Claus, with a Christmas fern for background, is the feature attraction of a simple holiday scene, staged in a 6-inch candy jar. Any available sprig with berry can be used to deck out the foreground. The fern is growing in soil, while gravel gives texture contrast to the colorful figurine.

Make your own. You may not find a shapely little tree that fits into a glass container. In which case, cut 2 heavily-needled balsam twigs to a length that will fit the container, allowing a generous margin at the top and sides. Wire the twig ends tightly together; soak them for 24 hours in a Christmas tree preservative to prevent needle drop. Then, insert the bound ends in a needled flower-holder stuck to the bottom of the container with clay. Trim the branches, and conceal the holder with dried decorator moss or colored aquarium gravel. You needn't water or cover.

FRAMED CHRISTMAS TREES FROM FERN FRONDS

Use the method described in chapter 8 for pressing some perfectly-shaped fern fronds. For about the right scale, locate a wooden picture frame approximately 5 by 7 inches. Use rubber cement to glue the frond onto a background piece of construction paper, but place it so that you leave at least a ¾-inch margin between both top and bottom of your frond and the frame itself: you'll need this room for a Christmas star at the top and a small paper tub underneath. "Pot" the tree in the tub, crown it with the star (a gummed seal, of course) and then trim it with colorful sequin ornaments which you dip in glue and apply to the pinnule branches with a stamp tongs. You can color the tub as you like, but the old-fashioned tree with multi-colored ornaments potted in a red tub remains the people's choice.

AROUND THE CALENDAR AND MISCELLANEOUS GIFT OCCASIONS

Plastic hearts used as candy boxes make most apt *Valentine's Day* planters and display cases for floral tokens (after the candy's been eaten). Mount your whatevers on a chip of bark or driftwood, and glue; fill the hearts with twigs, grasses and ferns; they make poignant keepsakes. You needn't be Irish to give a glass bowl filled with shamrocks for *St. Patrick's Day.* For *Easter,* use a crystal egg (see Sources of Supply) as a perfect container for a bright-faced viola; plastic eggs emptied of their original jellybean contents can be filled with blossoms.

Resurrection Gardens

If you have a good-sized terrarium, create a rocky grotto suggesting the empty tomb, and plant around it. Every flower that grows anew is, by definition, suggestive of the Easter rebirth theme, but the Jack-in-the-pulpit and lily-of-the-valley are legendary flowers particularly associated with the festival. The Jack-in-the-pulpit, it's said, received its markings from Christ's blood on Calvary, and the lily-of-the-valley supposedly sprouted from Mary's tears. An angel from your Christmas Crèche is an appropriate figurine.

Thanksgiving lends itself to a bottle garden, or an appropriate harvest arrangement of dried grasses and berries. *Baby bottles,* complete with rubber nipples (unlikely as this sounds!) make whimsical planters for a new mother or a baby shower. Add to the spirit of the occasion with a tiny plastic baby doll or a stork. *For the men,* a glass garden set in a wine decanter, whiskey bottle or old tobacco jar strikes the appropriately masculine gift note that some may feel cut flowers lack. And for *shut-ins, hospital patients and convalescents,* the glass garden gift is both spirit-lifting and genuinely practical: it takes up little bedside space, doesn't require arranging or watering; no busy nurse needs to find a vase for it; sealed containers don't compete for oxygen and can remain in the sickroom; there is no irritating fragrance; above all, you can bring the patient a bit of the outdoors to divert him. Medicine and plastic pill bottles offer unlimited possibilities, and by way of harmless amusement, you can stage the planting in a bottle identical to the one the patient's own medication comes in.

A complete terrarium kit—moss, soil, pebbles, plants, tools, container—the works—is an absorbing and manageable gift for an incapacitated convalescent who's chafing at his idleness, and children are enchanted by terrarium landscapes: maintaining a huge tank planter for an entire children's ward to enjoy is an exemplary work project for an ambitious garden club.

GLASS GARDENS AS FUND-RAISERS

Try the assembly-line procedure. Many hands make swift work. With a quantity of containers and the necessary tools, soil and plant material, a group can turn out a large crop of planters in a short time. Use a completed terrarium as a model, and follow the same planting procedure for each. Example: a 6-inch apothecary jar will need: 1½ inches of growing medium; a moss cup 6 inches in diameter; a

5-inch conifer seedling (or a fern, shining club moss or spotted pipsissewa of the same size); a half dozen partridgeberries and a rattlesnake plantain or strawberry begonia for the central feature; moss
and gravel for fill-in patches.

Spread the works out on a large table, and, with worker no. 1
inserting the moss liner, carry on down the line until the job's done,
the bottle watered, cleaned and corked — and the whole collection
ready for sale at the bazaar. Compiling and typing instructions to
accompany each planter will occupy the non-gardener in the group.
(There's always one in every crowd.) Make certain that you assemble all glass gardens intended for sale sufficiently in advance—several weeks, in fact—to give you ample time to check on how it functions.

You can mass-produce dried arrangements in the same fashion;
it's no problem to gather enough plant material for grand-scale bottle
stuffing when you grow your own (see the section on "Growing Material for Dried Arrangements from Seed" in chapter 8). Seed catalogs
list a large selection of annual everlastings and ornamental grasses,
many available in mixtures if you want to mix (see Sources of Supply).

10.

AQUATIC GARDENS, WITH OR
WITHOUT FISH

THE UNDER-WATER SCENE

"Aquarium" connotes fish, does it not? Tanks filled primarily with goldfish, gliding sinuously through undulating greenery. But, like the terrarium whose inner life occasionally includes small animals (see chapter 11 on this subject) as well as vegetation, your aquarium can be filled with vegetation for decorative purposes only. Try an aquatic garden, adding fish or not, as you please. It's a refreshingly cool sight during the summer dogdays, and in the winter, at the very least, it's a token Poor Man's Substitute for a Tropical Vacation. So much for the commercial.

In earlier days, aquarium plant life filled a functional necessity, that of supplying oxygen for the fish. Today this task is performed by modern aerators, and your plant selection can be guided entirely by beauty rather than utility. Look for pleasing plant forms; the one concession you'll want to make to your fish tenants, if you have them, is to provide them with several secluded plant hiding places.

PLANT MATERIAL

Although there are native pond plants that can be grown successfully in aquariums, the real aquatic naturals are the tropicals: floating, bunch, and root plants. I'll tick some of them off briefly: *eel grass, banana plant, arrowhead,* and *parrot's feather*: all good to look at. *Duckweed, hairgrass* and the root masses of the *water hyacinth* (oval leaves and blue blossom spikes) provide floating refuge for the small finned inhabitants. For an authentic poolside look, you can surround the tank with pots of *Equisetum* and *umbrella palm*.

Water Lilies

Two lovely aquarium bloomers warrant special mention: *Margaret Mary,* a tropical, is the first water lily to grow in an aquarium the year round. It's a miniature day bloomer, with blue flowers and a yellow center. It's viviparous, producing tiny newborn plants in the center of mature leaves. Second, *Dorothy Lamour* is a versatile lily with smooth-edged leaves on brilliant green stems, and rosebud flowers of brown and lemon-yellow.

PLANTING THE AQUARIUM

1. Wash *aquarium gravel* to remove dust; spread several inches on the bottom of the tank, sloping slightly upwards toward the rear. 2. Add *rocks* to the underwater seascape. Suit your fancy if the garden's for plants only, but if fish are present, exclude stones with mineral content. 3. Place a *newspaper* over the gravel, and gently pour in *water* until the tank is about one-third full. 4. Remove the paper. 5. Set in the *rooted plants,* covering them only to the topmost roots. 6. Remove the metal bands that hold *bunch plants* together, and bury the stems in gravel. 7. Now add more water, but not above elbow depth. After the water's cleared, you may want to move things around; no reason why not.

Left: *Amazon sword plant* (Crypto-coryne) *is featured in the cookie jar; a bit of coral and a whelk shell add decorative interest.* Right: *A clump of eel grass* (Vallisneria) *ascends the height of the wine bottle, with some suitably small pebbles clustered at its feet.*

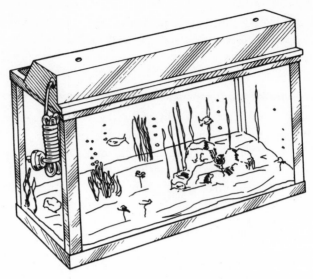

As a rule of thumb for aquarium lighting, two 20-watt tubes or one 40-watt Gro-Lux tube of light per gallon of water will insure good penetration of light in the water. Ten to twelve hours of light per 24-hour period, utilizing the wattage, will result in satisfactory plant growth and adequately supply the light requirements of fish.

AQUARIUM CARE

Light. Aquatic plants need light, but too much sunlight will cause algae to form on the glass. Supply artificial light with white fluorescents burned from 4 to 8 hours, depending on how much natural light the aquarium receives.

Temperature. With fish: 75° water temperature; plants only, 65°.

Placement. Aquariums don't have the mobility of terrariums. Aquatic gardens require caution and care; the collapse of a heavy water-filled tank could be disastrous, not merely in terms of loss of fish and plants, but the wrecking of furniture and costly rugs. Make certain you are using sturdy supports. Water weighs more than 8 pounds a gallon; a 5-gallon tank will add 40 pounds of weight for you to consider.

Coverage. Most fish tanks are equipped with metal reflectors that

cover half if not all of the top. Otherwise, cut a cover of glass or of plastic. Aquatic gardens with no fish needn't be covered at all.
Chores. Very few, especially if the garden is fishless. There are no feeding schedules and the tank will stay clean. You can limit your gardening responsibilities to scraping algae off the glass occasionally, and trimming or removing fast-growing vegetation. Add water to compensate for loss because of evaporation, preferably water that has stood for several days.

SMALLER AQUATIC GARDENS

For real live fish, use only the tank aquarium. The smaller rounded containers commonly termed fishbowls, can in fact be actual death traps for fish. They do, however, make fine settings for water plants, so use the so-called fishbowl as an addition to your houseplant displays.

A brandy snifter, landscaped with stones and gravel, makes a fine container for eel grass and parrot's feather. A series of vari-shaped aquatic garden containers will constitute an intriguing display on a window sill, providing needed moisture in dry rooms.

Jars and bottles of aquatic vegetation are decorative as well as practical: they lend moisture to the dried-out atmosphere of heated rooms and help the neighboring potted plants.

11.

JUNIOR TERRARIUM: *Play,*

Pastime, Pets and Projects

Few kinds of window-shopping are as rewarding as gazing into a glass garden. Shop windows, after all, change only once a week— but the living world inside a terrarium is in a constant state of flux. To start with, there are plants to watch, touch, smell and study. All the mysteries of green growth are contained in a small enclosed terrain, complete with its own environment and climate. And the vivarium, or terrarium garden that also houses small pets, is another dimension of glass gardening with enormous appeal for young observers. This chapter touches on those aspects of gardens in glass that make them absorbing objects of diversion and study for junior enthusiasts of all ages.

THINGS TO WATCH

SPROUT BOWLS FOR BEGINNERS

These are fast, and couldn't be simpler. All you do is sprinkle seeds —grass, clover, rye, peas, beans or lentils—into a bowl spread with several inches of moist sphagnum moss. The action follows fast. Cover the bowl, and keep it in a warm dim place until the seeds come up. Then move the sprout garden into the light. Admit air frequently by tilting the cover and removing it entirely if the seed begins to mold. When the plants become long and straggly, pull them out, and start another crop. You can use leftover flower and vegetable seeds, too, but they tend to take longer than the rapid-fire species listed above.

THE BEANSTALK, WITH OR WITHOUT JACK

Drop the seed of a climbing bean into a mossy glass bowl. And cover the bowl, not with glass, but with plastic; the bean, growing up, up and still up in an eager thrust for light (phototropism), will grow right out of the bowl. Make a slit in the plastic cover to accommodate it; then patch up the cover again with transparent tape. Because vines haven't the strength to hold their leaves erect, insert a stick, and tie the clambering beanstalk to it with string.

ROOT-GAZING

Watch the threadlike, elliptical wanderings of roots windowed in a tall, thin transparent bottle. Pack it firmly with enriched potting soil, moisten, and plant several seeds on the soil surface. Watch the roots (you'll see them as they develop against the sides of the bottle) as they proceed inexorably in a spiraled boring action called circumnutation. With a pencil, poke a pebble in the path of a root, so as to divert it from its determined course. The root will spiral right on down.

This same tenacious adhering to its predestined path can be observed with an *acorn*. Drop a ripened acorn into a terrarium, and learn how mighty oaks are born. The germinating acorn will split in half, one sprout thrusting upward as the trunk, the other pointing downward, forming the very beginning of the vital root system. Try reversing the sprouts. You'll find that the trunk sprout, now pointed downward, will about-face and persevere in growing skyward, while the roots will reverse as well, resuming their earthward probe.

QUIET: PLANTS SLEEPING

This is for the nightwatch. It's fascinating to observe the sleep (or nastic movement) of plants that fold their leaves at night. Included among these nocturnal drowsers are the sensitive plant, the prayer plant, and the *Oxalis* or wood sorrel, this last being particularly easy to observe. Closing time varies according to the temperature and the length of the day. My own vigilance has been rewarded by seeing clear changes in the position of a leaf at five and ten minute intervals, although I've never actually seen one move.

It is believed that this folding back of the leaves at night serves to protect the plant from loss of heat by radiation. Charles Darwin devoted considerable time to studying the reaction of *Oxalis* leaves to light.

THE INSECTIVORES: DEADLY BUG-EATERS AT WORK

We think of plants as being used for food by hungry creatures on the prowl, but not vice versa. Well, the terrarium presents us with an opportunity to watch the weird feeding habits of a group of plants that subsist, at least in part, on live insects. These plants don't find essential nitrates and phosphates in their native habitats (usually acid sphagnum bogs), and so they receive their protein supplement by consuming insects attracted by various trapping devices. These bug-trapping plants are global, and there are several North American species available to American gardeners. Actually, carnivores don't absolutely require the intake of insects as provender, but, like fertilizer for certain houseplants, it does promote healthy vigorous growth, and should be encouraged: invite insects by removing the terrarium cover twice a month, but supplement this catch-as-catch-can method by handfeeding your cannibalistic specimens with insects you've caught yourself. During the winter, supply the sundew and Venus's flytrap (see below) with an alternate diet of meat scraps, which you place on the leaves with tweezers. Don't overfeed; these plants are accustomed to working for their dinner.

Rear the insect traps together with other terrarium plants that share their need for acid unenriched soil and sphagnum. They thrive on ample sunlight, and the abundant moist humidity provided by covered terrariums. Although insect trapping is their most interesting scientific, plant-in-action specialty, these versatile insectivores offer an additional bonus of blossoms as well.

Insectivores available for your terrarium laboratory include:

Pitcher plants

This group includes the northern pitcher plant, the related southern huntsman's horn, and the Pacific Coast *Darlingtonia,* sometimes called the cobra orchid. They are equipped with tubular-shaped leaves that contain protein-digesting enzymes and bacteria. This fluid, mixed with rainwater, forms a lethal concoction that drowns insects and digests them into the plant system. Bristling, downward-curving hairs prevent trapped victim from escaping.

Venus's flytrap

A botanical mystery, this plant is equipped with a two-lobed leaf edged with curved bristles, which snaps shut in a fraction of a second around the unsuspecting prey. A single plant may contain as many as a dozen traps. They are triggered off at the slightest stimulus by what some botanists believe is an electrical action.

Flypaper traps

This group includes the *sundews,* sticky and deadly, whose leaf tentacles secrete both mucilaginous and digestive enzymes that reduce a housefly to pulp. The digestive process takes several days; then the leaf tentacles resume their open position, and the traps are in business again. *Butterworts* go about their destructive enterprises in a similar fashion; their leaves, better described as buttery rather than sticky, fold their margins over their victims in a clinging, deadly embrace. (For further data on insectivores/carnivores, see the Plant Encyclopedia, section 2, "Houseplants.")

CRYSTAL GARDENS: A FISHBOWL FULL OF STALAGMITES

In the early 1930s, lean years for almost everyone, "crystal gardens" made from lumps of coal were so popular that they came to be called "Depression Gardens." They're just as simple, inexpensive and fantastic today; here's what you do: Put several lumps of coal (bits of broken cinder block can be used instead) in the bottom of a fishbowl. Next, make a mixture of 4 tablespoons apiece of laundry bleach and ammonia water, and pour it over the coal. Pouring from the side, add more solution at intervals of several days. The chemical reaction is spectacular. You can obtain similar results by buying a magic underwater crystal garden, following the directions on the box, and see the crystals erupt into grotesquely colorful stalagmites that fill the fishbowl.

THE VIVARIUM: PETS LIVE HERE

Take a good-sized terrarium, plant it in natural landscape style, and move in some small friends, whose number may include turtles, salamanders, crickets, chameleons, toads and even snakes. As pets must have air, the glass covering should not fit snugly; allow an inch of ventilation at either end. However, because some of your domesticated pals may get wanderlust, cut wire screening the size of the entire opening and place the glass cover over it. Because the vivarium is constantly ventilated, moisture will escape and the plants will need watering. Needless to add, food and water must be provided regularly for the tenants, too.

TURTLES

The small green-shelled turtles displayed in petshops by the tankful do not belong in low, squat turtle bowls. They were created to inhabit the marshy margins of a pond. This is the environment you'll want to duplicate. So plan your turtle garden around a shallow plastic bowl from 1 to 2 inches deep, placed so that it's easily removed for

Vivarium: Turtles live here. *Plant a tank terrarium for turtles (or other small pets) as you would ordinarily, except that plants are relegated to the back and sides, leaving a large central area of pebbles, rock and moss for sunning. The all-important feeding pool is a pair of shallow matching plastic bowls, one fitted inside the other. The bottom bowl stays put in the landscape; remove the inner bowl for cleaning, and you won't disrupt the landscape. Offer the turtles access to their pool via a flat sloping rock.*
An umbrella palm and wood fern provide a touch of jungle; shining club moss and living sphagnum are planted in the foreground. The pool is rimmed with strips of sheet moss, easily replaced after cleaning. Because the terrarium cover must be left open at both ends to provide air for the pets, you should give the plants an occasional light sprinkling.

water-changing and cleaning. Follow the usual terrarium procedure of lining with moss, adding soil and charcoal, and sloping the soil upwards from the foreground pool: make a little mountain peak molded from stones. Plant ferns, small evergreens, and miniature palms. Don't plant anything permanent around the pool itself; set it into the soil, and cover the rims with moss and flat stones. Put a few stones into the water for the turtles to climb on. Terrarium turtle fare consists of insects, ant eggs and bits of meat; you can buy commercial turtle food as well. Give your shell-backed friends plenty of sun; they're avid sunbathers.

Here's a special suggestion for easing your pond-tending chores. Try the stacking, or pond-within-a-pond, method. Take, for example, two plastic dishes or bowls; plant one of them securely into the landscape, for keeps. Then insert the second one inside it, as in stacking icebox dishes on the shelf, and use this unplanted pond for easy removal and insertion when cleaning and water-changing are in order. A simple-minded notion, but it really makes things much easier.

SALAMANDERS

The salamander differs from the lizard in that it has smooth skin instead of scales, and toes instead of claws. Some 135 varieties of these tailed amphibians that resemble monsters from a prehistoric age can be found in the United States. Often, while digging about for plants in the woods, I turn over a salamander. They're often found, too, amid the broken glass and rusted cans of old dumping sites that offer so many hiding places.

Your most likely vivarium applicant among the salamanders is the newt, a cross between an aquatic and land creature. The newt spends several months in the water in the larval stage; once hatched, it moves onto dry land, clad in a spotted rusty red skin. During this colorful life phase, it is known as a red eft. Next transformation: it develops a broader tail for swimming, changes color again, and returns to the water for the balance of its life—from terrarium to aquarium. During their earth or red eft period, newts do most of their hunting under the cloak of night, as their bright color makes them an easy target for birds and other predators.

Provide lots of hiding places for salamanders in your garden. You'll probably need a flashlight to locate them at night. Their smooth skin makes them sensitive to sun, so give them the protection of shade-loving plants. Feed them on mealworms and small live insects, dropped in a saucer of water.

THE HORNED TOAD

This is a creature of the desert, and it shares with plants from similar areas an affinity for dry heat. So, for these desert denizens, a terrarium home must be warm and dry. Plant it, therefore, with cactus and similar desert plants. Allow the cover to be open at both ends, which means occasional waterings. The horned toad is actually a lizard, and in spite of his monstrous appearance, he's quite harmless: his scaly getup is his protective armor against the glaring desert sun. Up against it, he'll flatten himself out rather than pick a fight. His most frightening trait is to eject a stream of blood from his eye slits when he's disturbed. He's not accustomed to a rich diet; in his native habitat, he's restricted to such meager fare as he can procure with the lightning action of his tongue: ants, grubs, grasshoppers and the like. He'll be pleased with mealworms, too. If it's cold, he'll lose his appetite. The female of the species bears live young, which forage about on their own soon after they're born. Horned toads like to burrow away long before sunset, so provide rocky crevices in your landscape.

INSECT PETS

The sound of music is added to the terrarium with the acquisition of chirping *crickets,* and most interesting pets they are; the Chinese have caged them for centuries. They are strictly summer romances, however; they don't survive more than a month or so indoors after cold weather comes; their tissues freeze when the temperature drops below 32°. I've never kept one beyond mid-December.

A few tufts of grass in the landscape will satisfy crickets' food needs, but if the spirit moves them, they'll cheerfully devour table scraps and even one another. If you've housed several crickets together, offer an occasional bit of meat as a safeguard against their cannibalistic tendencies. DO NOT turn a cricket loose in a terrarium containing choice plants: the defoliation that ensues will be slow, but thorough. And this affable insect is equally destructive to household goods such as slipcovers, draperies, rugs and upholstery. Try to keep him fiddling away inside his glass garden, where he'll seek out a rocky crevice or burrow under the moss. Nocturnal creature though he is, he'll nevertheless enjoy sunning himself in the entrance to his den. (The female of the species, by the way, does not chirp, a sound-effect peculiar to the male that's actually produced by a fiddlelike scraping of the wings. The ladies have a central tail-like ovipositor designed for laying eggs in the ground.

Praying manties won't defoliate the terrarium, but they may consume one another. Their chief positive contribution to the scheme of things is that they combat insect crime, devouring insect pests avidly, among them the Japanese beetle. It's fun to watch the frothy egg masses hatch into a creeping colony, but they belong outdoors.

TERRARIUM PROJECTS FOR CLASSROOMS

COLLECT:

(1) Specimens of such woodland, aquatic, desert and houseplants (both flowering and foliage) as grow around the school, in addition to slips from the houseplants at home. Define and discuss all findings.

(2) Leaves of trees, shrubs, garden flowers, blossoms and seedpods from plants in the neighborhood (only with owners' approval). Press them according to the directions on "Dried Arrangements under Glass"; label them, and arrange a display. Or,

(3) Plastic containers, fill them with the pressed specimens again as described in the "Dried Arrangements" chapter, and bring them home as gifts.

(4) Natural materials, such as shells, stones, rocks, sand, and pebbles that fit into the terrarium the group is working on.

(5) Discarded glass bottles with sufficiently large openings for bottle-garden work. Bring them into class scrubbed and ready to use, together with corks or covers.

(6) Moss and soil for potting. Buy or bring in seeds and then see "4" just below.

UNDER GLASS:

(1) Using materials collected in (4) above, create a vivarium for frogs, turtles, toads or salamanders, as described earlier in this chap-

ter, not forgetting the importance of resting and hiding places.

(2) Divide up into groups; let each group grow a different kind of plant under glass, using containers brought in by members of the class.

(3) Have each group set up an experimental control, creating conditions of overwatering, underwatering, proper and improper care, and then demonstrating the results to the rest of the class.

(4) Use the materials collected in (6) above, using the information given in the "Terrarium as Nursery" chapter. Allow plenty of time for the seeds to sprout; once they've become seedlings, transfer them to plant the glass bottles that people have brought in.

There are dozens more. Dream them up!

12. A PLANT ENCYCLOPEDIA

By and large, I've selected for this encyclopedia those plants that respond favorably to moist terrarium conditions. Salient exceptions are cacti and certain succulents (to which I've devoted a sub-section), which should be grown in drier and usually unsealed containers. Also, I've kept in mind the restrictions on size imposed by most gardens in glass, indicating when robust growth may make transplanting necessary.

It goes without saying, but I'll say it anyway, that for any given garden in glass, you'll want to choose your plants in terms of their compatibility. Size, of course, is of paramount importance; plants must be scaled to the container and to one another. Light is another determining factor; you can't house shade-loving ferns and palms under the same sealed lid with a batch of plants that thrive in hot sunlight. *However,* keep in mind that plants can usually tolerate both greater and lesser amounts of light than those advocated here as ideal. You'll find that shade addicts won't be blighted by brief encounters with sunlight; many of our native plants, although classified as summer shade plants, do actually flower in the warm spring sun.

And although moisture needs are another criterion of compatability (you won't bed down a plant that craves humidity with ones requiring arid desert conditions) the fact is that most of these plants *are* moisture-loving, and as such are all-purpose terrarium candidates.

Plants that grow rapidly should be reared only in containers with ample openings that permit easy access for pruning and/or removal. Rule of thumb: what goes in must come out, and keep in mind that what goes in may grow a lot bigger during its under-glass sojourn than it was when you first neatly maneuvered it there.

To revert for the last time to the matter of soil: plants with specific soil preferences can't possibly perform at their best, even though they may survive, in a general-purpose potting mixture—so note the soil specifications given here, and don't hesitate to dig up additional information elsewhere. John Dewey it was who once said that man is essentially like a chemical: in certain environments, he is prone to turn green. The great educator was, of course, speaking figuratively and psychologically. Well, in certain uncongenial environments, plants that *should* be turning green proceed to wither. To each, his natural and most benign habitat, and that's why I've gone to repetitive lengths to indicate propitious growing conditions for the terrarium plants we're dealing with.

By all means broaden your glass gardening horizons beyond the confines of these pages: try moisture-loving plants indigenous to your own neighborhood, as well as the newer nursery catalog suggestions. Like me, you're certain to find your own favorites.

There were many ways in which I might have categorized the plants, but I fixed upon the three main sections that follow—garden plants, houseplants and woodland plants—as the overall plan; subsections occasionally cross these main boundaries, but when they do, you are given the necessary cross-reference. Any and all of the plants, regardless of category, can be bought; many can be found; a large percentage you can propagate yourself, using the various methods suggested here.

Finally, I've listed the plants under their common or best-known names because I felt that the encyclopedia would be most useful and accessible to you compiled in this way.

Garden Plants

Clumps of garden flowers, unnoticed in the comparative vastness of the outdoor landscape, acquire stature, interest and importance in the terrarium. My favorite plants for this double-duty performance are listed in the pages that follow. Generally, they must be dug up before the ground freezes. If interim storage is necessary, set them into a coldframe protected by a light covering of hay or pine needles and water them occasionally. They can then be moved into a glass garden in a cool sunporch or north window to ease the transition, as a steam-heated living room may be too hot to serve as their first indoor habitat. (For more detailed discussion on transplanting, see "The Terrarium as Nursery," chapter 10.)

BUGLEWEED—*Ajuga* (adj'oo-ga) *reptans*

Lift this plant from your rock garden, give it some shade, and it will reward you with bluish-purple spiked flower clusters. You can also grow it from seed planted in ordinary terrarium soil, or root its stems.

CLOVER, see *Trifoliate Plants*

CONIFERS AND DECIDUOUS TREE SEEDLINGS

Because you may be in no position to roam the woods, and because these are all domesticatable trees found in gardens, I'm including them in the garden section. You may come upon a seedling under garden shrubbery; if you acquire one in the woods, put it in a moist, shady garden corner reserved for terrarium plantings.

Conifers

Most native and ornamental conifer seedlings can be included in background plantings or displayed individually in bonsai and saikei landscapes. They are most attractive when new growth tips the branches with soft contrasting tufts of greenery. The fernlike Canadian hemlock is my favorite terrarium tree, not merely because it's native to my locality, but because the graceful branches lend themselves particularly well to shaping.

Some native and ornamental species commonly available include: arborvitae, balsam fir, Canadian hemlock, red cedar, pine, spruce, and yew; pines, junipers and red cedar can tolerate drier and sandier growing conditions than can most of the other conifers.

If you buy your conifer at a nursery or other source of plant supply, it may well be sold to you with the roots almost devoid of soil. Plant it just as soon as possible in your terrarium, giving it ample soil-depth and surroundings, and you'll have no problem.

Deciduous seedlings

Those that are growable in the terrarium include elm and birch. If you dig them in the autumn, after their foliage has fallen, they'll leaf out anew in their own vernal season after a period of dormancy.

CREEPING LOOSESTRIFE—*Lysimachia Nummularia.* Primrose
    family, naturalized in Eastern United States.

A glossy-leafed creeping vine that grows to a height of 1 or more inches in the terrarium but sprawls in lengths of 6 inches to a foot or more. Yellow flowers are borne in the leaf axils.

CREEPING MYRTLE, see *Periwinkle*

CROCUS SIEBERI

An early-blooming garden favorite, this small-flowered species of crocus can be used for temporary color spots in cool but sunny glass gardens. Press the bulbs lightly into the soil, leaving the tops exposed; conceal these with moss until the plant's roots are firmly anchored; then remove the moss, exposing the sprouts to light. You'll have flowers in 6 to 8 weeks.

JAPANESE SPURGE—*Pachysandra terminalis*

This quick-spreading, palmlike evergreen foliage plant makes a fine covering for the terrarium terrain. It roots quickly and easily from cuttings, and can be started in large quantities in sand-filled terrarium nurseries for either indoor or outdoor planting. 'Silveredge' is a variegated form, distinguished by silvery-white leaf margins.

LILY-OF-THE-VALLEY—*Convallaria* (kon-va-lair′i-a) *majalis*

Who doesn't cherish the delicately perfumed, white, nodding flower of this plant? Dig your own, or buy ready-to-grow special forcing pips and keep them in cool, moist dormancy until midwinter. (See "The Terrarium as Nursery.") Then pull the clump apart and retain only the plumpest, most promising sprouts. (This is called the law of natural selection, isn't it?) The lily-of-the-valley has a horizontal rootstock, with upright buds and feeder roots attached to it. Trim these roots down to 3 inches and pack them in moist moss before you store them in a coldframe, sunless terrarium or refrigerator, where below-50° temperature will discourage premature sprouting. Then in February plant them indoors, where they'll impart temporary color and fragrance to a glass garden. The flowers are forced at normal Maytime blooming temperature, which is about 70°.

PERIWINKLE—*Vinca minor,* also called *Creeping Myrtle*

The shiny evergreen leaves on trailing wiry stems with pale blue blossoms are widely used as fillers or in blossom bowls. You can start indoor specimens by taking summer cuttings from young shoots in the garden, and planting them right in ordinary terrarium soil. Pinch the tops to make the plant bushy, if desired.

PRIMROSE—*Primula veris*

Primula means first, and it's applied to this popular blossom-bowl plant because of its early spring flowering. Any of the multicolored diminutive varieties may be lifted for forcing. Plant in rich garden soil generously mixed with leaf mold.

TRIFOLIATE PLANTS: Clover, Shamrock; see also *Wood Sorrel* in 3, "Woodland Plants."

Even Irishmen can't agree on which—the yellow-flowered *T. dubium minus* or the white *T. repens minus*—is the true shamrock, as both of these clovers grow abundantly in the Emerald Isle. They do agree, however, that it was the clover, and *not* the wood sorrel, that St. Patrick used to exemplify the Trinity to the pagan Celts.

Be all that as it may, these low, creeping perennials are grown from seed sprinkled on moist moss, and their rounded trifoliate leaves, in glass bowl displays, make welcome spring gifts.

VIOLET—*Viola odorata*

This is the domestic sweet violet. You can move it from your garden into a coldframe, and from the coldframe into winter blossom bowls. This is also "the florist's violet"; hybrids of the species that are suitable for forcing are 'Rosea', 'Royal Robe', 'Double Russian', 'Princess of Wales', 'White Czar', and 'Swanley White'.

Houseplants

AFRICAN VIOLET—*Saintpaulia*

Blue, white, purple and pink blossoms offer spectacular color for glass gardens: the African violet is natural star material for blossom bowls, and as a featured flower in any glass garden setting; the miniature varieties are tailored to terrarium size. Buy small new plants, as they respond more favorably to humidity than do older ones. You can also grow this flower from seed or from leaf cuttings. (See chapter 10, "The Terrarium as Nursery," section on houseplants from seed.)

Soil Sterilize soil, sand and leafmold by baking them for 1 hour at 180° as precaution against nematode infection.

Care Maintain a moist, humid atmosphere but one that is free of dripping moisture: prop up the terrarium cover with a match stem. Give warmth with ample light, but little direct sun. The plant is adaptable as to temperature and can take a fluctuation of from 60° to 75°. Water frequently so that the soil is moist but not sopping wet; use a can with a long spout so that water doesn't touch leaves or crown. Rainwater is preferred, and, in limestone regions where the water is hard, it's mandatory. Feed with African violet food, with diluted manure, or with 5-10-5 applied to damp soil every second week or so.

AGLAONEMA (ag-la-o-nee′mah)—*Chinese Evergreen,* also called *Chinese Waterplant, Japanese Leaf*

This long-leaved tropical houseplant grows easily in water, and thrives in the warm moist atmosphere of the terrarium. *A. simplex* has plain, dull green leaves; *A. treublii* is light green and creamy. It can be started from root divisions or pieces of leaf planted in moist sand or water. The rooted plant can then be set into terrarium soil. Keep it in a garden to which you've easy access, because the leaves grow to 10 inches or longer and require trimming. Potting mixture to which charcoal has been added is congenial soil.

147

ALUMINUM PLANT, see *Pilea cadieri*

ANTHURIUM *scherzerianum—Flamingo Flower*

The anthurium, a showy and striking plant, boasts brilliant flowers whose colors include bright shades of red, salmon, coral pink, or white. *A. scherzerianum* is a dwarf form discovered in Guatemala. Its long leaves measure about 8 by 2 inches. It requires moisture, warmth, and plenty of humidity. Keep it in partial shade; plant it in soil rich in humus, and cover the roots deeply.

AQUATIC   PLANTS—see chapter 10. WATER HYACINTH; WATER-LILY MINIATURES: *Margaret Mary; Dorothy Lamour*

ARALIA—*Dizygotheca* (dizzy-go-thee′ka) *elegantissima*

Narrow drooping leaves look like lacy fingers. This plant may quickly outgrow its site, so keep it in an accessible bottle or tank. When it gets too big for your glass garden, you'll want to pot it elsewhere for indoor decoration. It needs moderate humidity, the rather warm temperature of our overheated houses, as much daylight as you can give it, and plenty of water (soil should always feel or look wet).

ASPARAGUS FERN—*Asparagus plumosus*

This feathery and fernlike plant, widely grown by florists, is neither fern nor asparagus. It has whitish flowers and purple-black berries, and boasts an effective silhouette. It comes, too, in a dwarf version called *Nanus.* Asparagus ferns can be grown from seed; they need light, but not sunlight.

BABY'S TEARS—*Helxine soleiroli,* also called *Corsican Nettle*

An extremely delicate little plant, valuable for its mosslike and minute foliage.

BEGONIA, FIBROUS-ROOTED—*Begoniaceae* family, of which the begonia is the *only* genus!

Books have been written about this huge genus (about 1,000 species) of tropical foliage and flowering herbs; it's even got its own monthly magazine, *The Begonian*. Anyway, its polished leaves and riot of small flowers make it a lovely inmate for the terrarium, and, because of its preference for similar conditions, a good companion to such houseplant favorites as African violets, coleus, palms, and potted ferns. Try dwarf begonias, which rarely exceed 6 to 8 inches, for smaller gardens: 'Red Wonder', bright pink 'Linda', 'Rose Perfection', white-blossomed 'Viva', and 'Red Ball'. Bronze-leaved dwarfs include pink 'Steffi' and 'White Polly'. They can be grown from seed or from a slip set in terrarium soil.

Overly wet conditions could cause stem rot, so ventilate, if necessary, by lifting the terrarium cover. Soil should be moist, however. Temperatures ranging from 75° to 85° are suitable; give daylight, but only occasional direct sunlight.

The bright begonia, in addition to being a natural focal attraction and source of terrarium color, is well-suited for blossom bowls.

BERTOLONIA—*Melastomacae* family

A tiny sprawler with delicate silver-veined coppery leaves and minute flower clusters on upright stems. It thrives in dense shade and humidity, and increases readily from cuttings stuck in moist terrarium moss.

CACTI AND SUCCULENTS

What have cacti and succulents in common? All cacti are succulents but not vice versa. Both include varieties with spines, but spined plants aren't necessarily one or the other. The common denominator is that both are xerophytic—native to dry regions, and in order to exist without rainfall over a period of many months, they've adapted by developing a structure for storing moisture.

Succulents come from many families and places; they include the fleshy, water-storing aloes, the semperviviums, the sedums, and such plants as the snake plant or leopard lily.

Varieties of both cacti and succulents are fascinating for terrarium use. Echeverias, some sedums, and kleinias, none of which ever bloom, are small and have exquisite shadings of color. You'll use combinations of small cacti to create miniature desert scenes.

Off with the lid: most cacti and succulents are *not* grown in moist humidity, and you may plant them in uncovered fishbowls or brandy glasses, except for golden moss (*Sedum acre*), see below. Hot dry room temperatures suit most of them fine. They are prime candidates for open glass containers because not only do they look attractive, but because their shallow roots adapt readily to small areas. The open glass permits of easy watering; it shelters the plants from drafts, and discourages Junior's eager fingers from exploring the spiny specimens.

The fleshy varieties can be grown only in wide-open planters. Spread coarse gravel generously over the bottom, skipping the usual moss liner; then pour in the specially prepared cactus soil. You'll use tongs, I hope, to place prickly cactus. Scratch a hole for its roots with your trusty dowel, insert the plant, and pack the soil firmly around it. The desert ambiance is enhanced greatly by the use of a few pieces of Featherock.

But remember that not all cacti and/or succulents thrive on a dry, sunny growing environment, so once again, base your plant selection on cultural requirements. You can achieve a congenial terrarium by combining different kinds of pincushion, barrel, and flat padded opuntia cactus, sedums, crassulas, and echeverias.

Soil   Provide a soil that's porous but not poor; use 2 parts sand and topsoil with ½ part leaf mold. As most desert soils are alkaline, include some bone meal and ground limestone as well. Another dependable formula consists of equal amounts of potting soil, sand, and milled sphagnum. Drainage can be achieved by adding ⅓ vermiculite to the mix.

Care   Most desert soils are especially rich in minerals, so that the plants in this group that originate in arid regions should be given supplementary feeding. As spring growth begins, use cottonseed meal or hoof and horn meal as fodder. Avoid nitrogenous fertilizers, which force over-development of soft tissues.

Cacti-succulents, with the exception of the *Sempervivums* and the *Epiphyllums,* will take all the light you can provide. *Light,* that is; not *heat:* your brightest window doesn't mean your hottest or sunniest, because, oddly enough, these plants can actually become sunburned if the heat they receive through glass is too great. Also, their limited root systems can't withstand intensely hot sun. Do not include them in a terrarium placed on a radiator sill. The notable exception is the sun-resistant, spine-covered desert cactus.

Cacti and succulents in glass containers do well in a daytime high that never exceeds 75°, and a nocturnal temperature of 50°.

Most desert plants will require water about every ten days, although some less demanding species can go unslaked for three weeks. (Actually, most desert plants are not innately drought resistant; they've adapted, perforce, to their arid surroundings.) Most rotting is due to overwatering. Light but frequent watering will ensure moist, but not wet, roots. If the plant has a depressed crown, make certain that you water it from the side, not from the top. During their winter rest period, these plants can live successfully in somewhat drier soil.

CARNIVOROUS PLANTS

(see also "Junior Terrarium," section entitled "The Insectivores: Deadly Bug-Eaters at Work.")

Take a fifth-grade boy, introduce him to plants that capture insects for food and then drown, poison or crush their victims as part of the digestive process, and—instant fascination. Confined in a terrarium where the pickings aren't so good, these insect-eaters can do without such gustatory treats, but they'll do better if hand-fed every two months or so—with meat scraps instead of insects if you're squeamish, at least in the case of the sundew and the Venus's flytrap. Place the food on the leaves with tweezers rather than in plant cups. Don't overfeed these horticultural oddities in any case; their leaves will turn brownish as a symptom of an over-rich diet. They require an acid growing medium; use shredded sphagnum moss and no soil. Sand or vermiculite are possible alternatives. Provide abundant sunlight, but shade during the hot summer months. They require lots of humidity. For the most part, they need a temperature of 80°; at lower readings, they'll grow at a slower rate. Native pitcher plants become dormant with the first fall freeze.

PITCHER PLANTS

This group drown their prey in pitchers whose bottoms hold a watery liquid. *Sarracenia flava,* the southern pitcher plant, is a specimen with yellow-green leaves that grows to about 2 feet in height. *S. purpurea,* the northern pitcher plant, has hollow enlarged leaves that form pitchers striped in green, red, or yellow. In winter, the frozen cups look like boiled lobster claws. The insect-trapping leaves are the main attraction, but the flowers, resembling inverted red tulips on 12-inch stems, are also outstanding. Another member of the family is *Darlingtonia californica,* commonly called the cobra lily, or California pitcher plant; its water-filled leaves are shaped like a cobra's head. Red-veined green stems support yellowish green and red hoods. Come spring, reddish flowers appear.

SUNDEW   (*Drosera rotundifolia*) and Butterwort (*Pinguicula pumila*) (see also section 3, "Woodland Plants") belong to another group, and go about their lethal business by other means: they use sticky hairs for attracting and holding their prey, which is then killed and absorbed by plant secretion. The sundew has pinkish white blossoms borne on long stems.

VENUS'S FLYTRAP   (*Dionaea muscipula*).

This spectacular plant crushes its victims in a paw-like trap. It is sold as a bulb on the basis of age, the bigger traps, not unreasonably, coming from older bulbs. Nectar and brilliant red color attract the victim to a leaf-trap edged with hairs and hinged at the center; the trap is sprung as soon as the trigger hairs are touched. (You can activate the trapping mechanism with a pencil or toothpick.) Once the insect is eaten, the trap opens and the plant is ready for its next victim. Keep the plant in full sun to bring out deep red coloring; shield it, however, from midday sun in summer. White flowers appear in the spring.

CHINESE EVERGREEN, see *Aglaonema*

CHLOROPHYTUM (clow-roff'itum) *elatum*. Lily family.

Despite the fact that it has no widely-accepted common name, this proliferous plant, with fountainlike striped green and white foliage, is very popular. New plants root at the ends of its long stems.

COLEUS (koh'lee-us)

The leaves of this foliage plant are so myriad-colored and brilliant that its little flower spikes are secondary. The toothed leaves are marked in red, green, white, yellow or purple; some run from deep

Coleus (approximately half size)

gold to bronze to olive to copper. Cuttings can be taken in August from full-sized plants, and they'll root in 3 or 4 weeks. Give them good light. Because you'll want to pinch them out if they grow too lustily, plant them in bottles or tanks that give you easy access. Pinched-off top shoots can then be rooted in water to make new plants.

CROTON—*Codiaeum* (ko-di-ee'um)

Spectacular foliage plant, with small inconspicuous flowers. Its leaves run to white, reds and yellows. It likes moisture and shade; can be propagated by cutting. Temperature shouldn't go below 70° to 75° at night.

DUMB CANE—*Dieffenbachia picta. Araceae* family

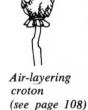

Air-layering croton (see page 108)

Mottled yellow and deep green foliage make this tall-growing tropical a good background selection for larger tanks and bottle plantings. However, the plant roots easily from cuttings, and small slips fit into less spacious planters too. Warmth, rich soil, and part shade are the preferences of this moisture-loving plant whose common name refers to its acrid juice, said to render one speechless.

ENGLISH IVY—*Hedera helix*

You know this evergreen! As it grows equally well in soil and water, it's a terrarium natural. Its preference include a cool temperature not in excess of 65°, light, and moisture. Sun is not desirable. Ivy is attractive in a bottle garden, and it's easy to propagate: just cut the stem, and insert it in water or sand.

FERNS, TROPICAL. (For other ferns, and general remarks on care and food, see section on "Woodland Plants".)

Especially popular are bird's nest fern (*Asplenium nidus*), an attractive bright yellow-green plant that makes a dramatic single display, and the sword fern, in particular the variety known as the Boston fern (*Nephrolepis exaltata bostoniensis*) which is considered the best of all house ferns.

Others suitable for terrarium use are the holly fern (*Cyrtomium falcatum*); the sword fern called *Nephrolepis cordifolia;* the most common of the tropical maidenhairs (*Adiantum cuneatum*) with its several varieties, one of which is commonly known as ocean spray; and the table fern (*Pteris crética*).

FLAMINGO FLOWER, see *Anthurium*

GLOXINIA—*Sinningia* (sin-ın gee-a) *pusilla*

Many varieties of gloxinia are too large for terrarium use—but *S. pusilla* is the baby of the family and a true miniature. Its long-tubed lavender leaves, striped with white, are slipper-shaped, and contrast with small puckered leaves of olive green. You can start it by planting tubers right in terrarium soil which should be rich and porous (equal parts of milled sphagnum moss, well-rotted leaf mold, rich garden loam, and clean sand). Leaf cuttings or seeds will produce flowering plants in about a year. Provide it with shade and constant warmth, with a minimum of 60° at night.

GOLDEN MOSS—*Sedum acre. Crassulaceae* family

A fleshy, creeping evergreen perennial with bright yellow blossoms that can be propagated from seeds, leaves, division of roots, or from cuttings taken in spring or summer. Use soil on the sandy side, and make free with sunlight. Moist humidity may cause this plant to straggle, so use it where you've easy access for removal or trimming.

HELXINE, see *Baby's Tears*

HOYA CARNOSA, see *Wax Plant*

KENILWORTH IVY—*Cymbalaria* (sim-ba-leh'ree-a)

This old-fashioned, dainty creeper can be grown from seeds dropped into a narrow-necked bottle. Although it's grown primarily for its foliage, you get an extra dividend in the yellow-throated, lilac-blue flowers. It's happiest in a cool glass garden, but it's flexible; give it moderate light, and little direct sun.

KOELLIKERRIA *erinoides. Gesneriad* family

A suggested terrarium-mate for *Phinaea multiflora* (see below), its close relative, this little plant produces a raceme of pink and white flowers 3 times the height of the 2-inch plant itself. As with Gloxinia, above, and other members of its family group, it needs rich porous soil, warmth, and some sun but not in abundance.

LEOPARD PLANT—*Ligularia* (lig-you-leh'reah)

This plant grows yellow and white blotched leaves on wooly stalks. You can start it either by making a cutting or by dividing the original plant. Eventually, it'll outgrow most tanks—but it's fun while it lasts. It likes ample light, but not sun.

NORFOLK ISLAND PINE—*Araucaria* (aw-row-keh'reah) *excelsa*
A graceful evergreen, with tiny pointed leaves curved at the tip. You can grow it from seed, or from the center leader of another plant. Provide it with moderate humidity, medium temperature (65° to 75°), as much daylight as possible but little direct sunlight; water it regularly but not excessively. This little pine, which can grow to a height of several feet in a pot, should obviously be used as a tree in a capacious terrarium.

ORCHIDS

From the innumerable types and varieties of orchids, I've selected for this encyclopedia a few particularly suitable for glass gardens. Three familiar orchid types that are easy to grow in even a small terrarium are the *Cypripediums,* whose lip is in the form of a pouch or shoe; the *Dendrobiums* with their lovely arching or pendant sprays of flowers of varying colors, and the *Cattleyas,* largest, best-known and most important of the orchid groups. The latter two categories are epiphytic, or air plants (see below); the *Cypripediums* are not.

Cypripedium parviflorum pubescens is the small yellow ladyslipper. Lacking water-storage organs, it needs more moisture than members of the other groups. Of the Cattleyas, *C. aclandiae* and *C. walkeriana* are popular. Also suitable for terrarium display are *Erythroides nobilis argyrocentrus,* or silver orchid, which needs adequate drainage, and *Epipactis repens* (*goodyera pubescens*), the rattlesnake plantain, a woodland orchid with veined, frosty green leaves growing from low rosettes that may produce 10-inch flower scopes. Also worth noting for orchid fanciers are *Lockhartia pallida, Paphiopedilum fairieanum* and *P. bellatulum;* grow them in pots of fern fiber or fir bark in a plantarium or tankstyle terrarium.

Soil Several different media are used for orchids. The epiphytic orchids (those that derive their needed moisture and nutrients from the air and rain—hence the apellation "air plant") are planted in osmundine fiber, a peaty material made from the ground-up roots of the osmunda fern. This fern fiber resists decay, and gives good ventilation and drainage. Also used is fir bark, which holds both moisture and plant food; there is ample air space between the chunks of bark. I recommend finely ground bark for seedlings, and coarser grades for larger, older plants. Finally, many growers use oak leaf mold over a bottom layer of coarse gravel. The terrestrial *Cypripediums* grow in a porous soil.

Care All orchids like early winter sunlight, but as the sun grows stronger, light must be filtered. Early morning and late afternoon sun is all that most orchids can take.

Orchids' temperature requirements vary, depending on the climatic conditions of their place of origin. Those that are native to cool growing areas enjoy a 50° thermometer reading; the intermediate group prefer 55°; those from more tropical habitats require an additional 10°.

Generally, and as you'd expect, orchids in covered glass planters need less water than those exposed to dry room temperature. However, because of the porous nature of their potting compositions, they can't be neglected as can other terrarium plants. Water them when the soil composition or fibrous fern roots feel dry. The roots of epiphytal orchids are bone white when dry; with too much water, they turn green. It's true that in their natural habitats, tropical orchids are subject to daily downpours, but it's equally true that the sun and wind soon dry them out. They do require humidity which is why they thrive in the Wardian case—but until you're sure, it's better to water too little than too much.

PATIENCE PLANT—*Impatiens sultani*

I. sultani is the smallest of this most popular and easily-reared genus.

It has smooth leaves and bright flowers (scarlet, pink, purple, white). Its only imperious demand is lots of moisture and either half a day's sun or direct bright light. It can grow as high as 2 feet, and may eventually have to be moved; it can be propagated by seeds or cuttings.

PEPPER PLANT—*Peperomia*

A handsome little tropical with glossy oval leaves. If it's kept moist and fed liquid manure on a more-or-less fortnightly basis, it should stay in fine condition. It needs moderate humidity, warm temperature, bright light and a fair amount of watering. It will root from cuttings, or even from cut leaves, which are set in sand and given bottom heat.

PHILODENDRON

This is an energetic, sprawling foliage plant that comes in dozens of species, many of which are extremely popular, and some small varieties of which you can buy at the five-and-ten, as we used to call it before inflation. But they do grow quickly, so be prepared to move them out of the terrarium when they grow too large, as, being hardy, they no doubt will. A porous soil containing peat moss is excellent. Philodendron will cheerfully tolerate high temperatures but not sunlight. Give them full light, however.

PHINAEA *multiflora. Gesneriad* family

Especially recommended for terrariums is this white miniature, whose tiny white flowers appear on top of medium green leaves when the plant is about one inch tall. Porous soil and temperature that doesn't drop below 60° are its requirements.

PILEA (pie'leah)—*Aluminum plant*

Fernlike leaves, silver-flecked and showy. Two species, *P. spruceana* and *P. cadieri minima,* are recommended for gardens in glass. You can start them by making cuttings above a leaf joint and inserting them in sand. Keep at 65°; roots will appear quickly, and when they do, transfer the cuttings to terrarium soil, and keep them moist. They like a partly shaded setting, and need little light—certainly not sunlight.

POTATO VINE—*Ceropegia woodii*. Milkweed family

This trailer makes fine foreground filler; use it, too, for cascading over rocky landscapes. It's produced from tubers—nodules which appear along the wire stems, interspersed with marbled heart-shaped leaves and tiny tubular flowers.

POTHOS—*Scindapsus* (sin-dap'suss) *aureus*, var. *Wilcoxii*

Its variegated, pale yellow leaf grows some 18 inches long and quite wide. Give it medium light, warm temperature and water it moderately; it can stand low humidity; it won't tolerate sun in direct form.

PRAYER PLANT—*Maranta leuconeura* (loo-kuh-noo'ra), var. *Kerchoveana*

Its handsomely mottled leaves, about 7" long and 3½" wide, are spotted underneath with chocolate-red markings (the plant's also known as rabbit's tracks). At night, the flat broad leaves fold together vertically, like a person's hands in prayer. Its white blossoms offer less interest than the leaves. Being bushy, it makes a good filler or background plant, and it will do well under most terrarium conditions.

SEDUM ACRE, see *Golden Moss*

SILK OAK—*Grevillea* (gre-vill'eah) *robusta*

Graceful, showy, fernlike leaves. Use as a specimen plant, for display, where the plant's height (2 to 3 feet) is appropriate. It needs a temperature of about 50° to 60° and plenty of light, but not direct sunlight.

SNAKE PLANT—*Sansevieria* (san-se-vee'ria), also called *Leopard Lily*

The straight, linear leaves contrast sharply with the mounded forms or rounded leaves of other houseplants. One species, *S. Hahni,* is low-growing, and its somewhat wider leaves are brilliantly marked. You can grow your own by cutting leaves into pieces and inserting the fragments in rather sandy terrarium soil. Or you can divide the root early in the spring and plant it in your terrarium. This plant likes some shade.

SNAKE PLANT
LEAF CUTTING

SPIDERWORT—*Tradescantia* (trayd'scan-cha) *virginiana alba,* also
  called *Inch Plant*

Watch this variegated creeper carefully, as it will inch its way into
every corner and usurp the entire terrarium if you leave it to its own
devices. You can buy the potted plant and set it in a terrarium soil,
or root it, easily, from either cuttings or pieces of stem set in soil. It
likes partial shade.

SPIKE MOSS—*Selaginella,* also called *Cushion,* or *Scotch Moss*

This moss-like, branching plant is a distinctive genus, differing from
true moss in that its stems and leaves contain tubular cells. Of its
hundreds of species, most are tropical, but some are native to North
America. It's taller and fluffier than real moss. *Emmeliana,* which has
ferny green foliage, is also called sweat plant because it thrives in
moist humidity. *Uncinata,* or rainbow moss, has leaves that reflect an
iridescent metallic blue. Both species grow rapidly from stems,
thrusting down stiltlike roots as the plant grows upward. These interesting spike mosses give good solo performances in individual
planters, as well as adding special foreground interest in the terrarium.

STRAWBERRY BEGONIA—*Saxifraga* (sak-siff'ra-ga) *sarmentosa,*
  also called *Strawberry Geranium, Aaron's beard,* or *Mother-of-
  Thousands.*

It's not a begonia, and it doesn't produce strawberries. A trailing
plant, it has fuzzy, silver-veined round leaves growing on rosy-colored
runners, at whose tips new plants form. You can root these by planting them in terrarium soil. The strawberry begonia is not a demanding
plant. It likes a fairly cool temperature (not above 65°) and light or
filtered sunlight. Keep its soil moist.

TOLMIEA (toll'me-ah) *menziesii,* popularly called *Piggy-back
Plant.* This popular houseplant has heart shaped leaves with toothed
edges. You can propagate the runners, which abound in summer, or pot
up the young plantlets, which you'll find where the leaf joins the stalk.
Use it in a shaded terrarium; it fits well, too, into a wild garden, but
may have to be removed when it grows to maturity.

TRAILING ARBUTUS—*Epigea* (epi-jee′a) *repens,* see section 3, "Woodland Plants".

UMBRELLA PLANT—*Cyperus* (sigh-peer′us) *alternifolius*

A slender-stemmed plant, growing umbrella-shaped clusters of leaves at stem-heights that range from 2-4 feet. You can start a new plant by setting the leaf crown in moist sand; it requires lots of moisture at the root. Give it a diet of light, unmixed with sun.

VIOLA TRICOLOR, popularly called *Pansy, Johnny-jump-up, Heartsease.*

This is the "little western wild flower" to which Shakespeare refers in "A Midsummer's Night Dream." It's the ancestor of our many pansy strains. Primarily, it needs part sun and summer shade, but it's flexible enough to be tolerant of full winter and early spring sunshine. The viola is a biennial, and it differs from most violets in that it produces leaves from branching stems. You can force it, in glass, from budded plants to obtain effective temporary color. As the viola blooms during winter thaws, it's content in a cool 60° temperature.

If you grow plants from seed, violas in combination offer delightful color variations on the tri-colored purple, yellow and white theme. Black imp, for example (*V. nigra*), is the rich color of dark velvet. Little Boy Blue is outstanding because of its pale-blue face and yellow centers.

WAX PLANT—*Hoya carnosa*

This plant, with its thick green waxy leaves, will do nicely in the terrarium. Its bonus is a sudden outcropping of pink, starlike blossoms. Give it humidity, living-room temperature, abundant light and heavy watering. Let it dry out slightly between downpours, but not to the point of aridity. The wax plant can be grown from seed which, sown in December, should bloom in July.

Woodland Plants

As with everything else, you can buy woodland plants. But you can also dig them. If circumstances permit, take off with your basket, trowel and/or shopping bag anytime you like. Vacations to other parts of the forest as well as local out-of-door meanderings can yield terrariumsful of native plants. Wherever you may live or visit, there's bound to be a moisture-loving wildling yearning to be transplanted to your glass garden. As simple an example as exists is the ubiquitous seedling evergreen—low, sprawling and all over the place. In earlier days, Main Street was bordered by woodland, and the sprouting off-shoots of our grandparents' common tree heritage can still be found in the wake of the suburban bulldozer.

So go plant-scrounging. You can collect plants as readily in December as in May; snag native woodland material any time except when it's covered with snow. Dig berries and such budded spring-flowering plants as arbutus in early autumn: if you wait too long, the birds'll have gotten the berries first.

Granted, very little of today's turf belongs to everyman; almost every parcel of land is somebody's private property: Keep Off, Do Not Trespass, Beware of the Dog. And when such is the case, don't waste your breath asking the owner's permission to pull up even so much as a weed.

Also, the statutes of many states list severe penalties (and may even invoke them!) for removing, without specific authorization, such plants as partridgeberry, bunchberry, wild lily-of-the-valley, winter-green, and other fruited plants vital to the sustaining of wildlife. Other plants protected by law are (among many) the trailing arbutus —the official floral emblem of the Commonwealth of Massachusetts as well as of the Province of Nova Scotia, and the mountain laurel, sacred (legally at least) to Connecticut and Pennsylvania.

Therefore, Admonition #1: check conservation lists carefully. Let off-limit plants be, no matter how alluring. This goes, too, for those field and wayside flowers you'd like to preserve for dried bouquets. Their seedheads are needed on location, to perpetuate the

161

species. (See relevant comments on moss in this section.) #2: Gather only those plants that are growing in abundance. #3: Take only what you need, and carefully re-cover such roots as you may have disturbed in the course of your excavations. #4: Use a trowel, and try to get a root ball whenever possible. #5: Carry plants in moistened plastic bags (see "The Voyaging Collector" in chapter 2). #6: If you're traveling by car, *don't* place your newly-dug treasures near the heat.

One matter about which we can generalize, regarding the plants treated in this section, is soil: woodland plants thrive in a mixture consisting of equal parts of leafmold, milled sphagnum and sand.

BOG WINTERGREEN—*Pyrola uliginosa*

Rounded oval leaves and pink blossoms make this a showy terrarium plant. Give it part shade and acid soil.

BUTTERWORT—*Pinguicula*

Small stemless insectivorous plant, with flat leaves. The solitary flowers are yellow, purple or white. The butterwort is often found in sphagnum moss; it likes shade and moisture, and a cool-to-moderate temperature. It propagates by seeds or division of plants.

CLAYTONIA virginica, see *Spring Beauty*

CLUB MOSSES—*Lycopodium*

These evergreen fern allies, technically not true mosses, form dense carpets in our acid-soiled eastern and northwestern woodlands. Some species are native to Europe and Asia. Several of the club mosses merit a glass gardener's attention, but most varieties, such as the sprawling ground cedar (*L. complanatum*) and the running club moss (*L. clavatum*) are usable only in larger gardens. Ground pine, or tree club moss (*L. obscurum*) is recommended for background, and, in saikei settings, for individual display. Graceful as the elms of New England's Main Streets, it has long provided background accompaniment for that Yankee favorite, the partridgeberry.

Shining Club Moss (approximately half size)

Shining Club Moss—*L. lucidulum*—is a versatile filler with many landscaping uses. It roots easily from cuttings.

COOLWORT, see *Foamflower*

CREEPING SNOWBERRY—*Chiogenes hispidula*. Heath family

Trailing aromatic evergreen shrub with bell-shaped flowers and white berries.

DWARF WAKEROBIN, see *Trillium nivale*

EARLY SAXIFRAGE—*Saxifraga* (saks-iff'ra-ga) *virginiensis*.

A plant that produces 4-inch to 9-inch white flower cymes from 3-inch basal rosettes. For drier and more airy planters.

FERNS

Ferns are almost indispensable auxiliaries; I rarely plant a landscape without them. But they can be a garden world unto themselves as well: their frond range includes the feathery, the leathery, the sharply defined, and the solid. This contrast in leaf patterns can make a bowlful of ferns emerge a highly dramatic presentation.

There is something exotic about the fragile fern frond; its graceful form makes flowers superfluous, and even if it were suddenly to sprout spectacular blossoms, I can't imagine that its inherent beauty would be enhanced. Henry Thoreau, that keen-eyed naturalist with the probing pen, wrote that "nature made ferns for pure leaves."

Look for all manner of ferns in the moist woods. ("Fern," by the way, is a generic, all-embracing term that covers most of the great American backyard flora.)

You can amass a collection of native evergreen ferns anytime, but deciduous plants must be dug before their foliage succumbs to the first frost.

Be they from temperate or tropical forests, most of the many thousand species of fern all share a need for moisture. They're hard to grow in dry hot apartments and living rooms, but they do very well in the humid atmosphere of the terrarium (remember that one of Dr. Ward's first specimens was a fern), and "fernarium", to many growers, is synonymous with "terrarium."

Whether you acquire native evergreen, native deciduous, or tropical florist's ferns, your problem will be to find specimens small enough for the containers you plan to use. The lists that follow are compiled with terrarium restrictions in mind.

NATIVE EVERGREEN FERNS: Christmas fern (*Polystichum acrostichoides*); rattlesnake fern (*Botrychium virginianum*); rock-cap fern (*Polypody virginianum*); leather grape fern (*Botrychium multifidum*); black-stemmed or ebony spleenwort (*Asplenium resiliens*); wood fern (*Dryopteris*), and walking fern (*Camptosorus*).

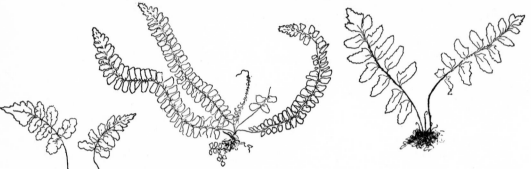

Ferns shown are shown approximately half size: Common wood fern. Ebony spleenwort. Christmas fern.

NATIVE DECIDUOUS FERNS: beech fern (*Dryopteris phegopteris*); bladder fern (*Cystopteris*); blunt-leafed cliff fern (*Woodsia*); cliff brake (*Pellaea*); lady fern (*Athyrium felix femina*); the lovely Northern maidenhair fern (*Adiantum pedatum*); oak fern (*Dryopteris currania*); royal fern (*Osmunda regalis*); sensitive fern (*Onoclea sensibilis*).

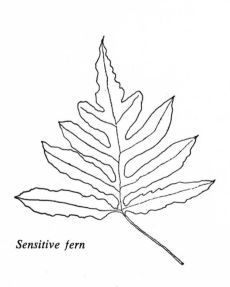

Sensitive fern

Common woodsia fern

TROPICAL FLORIST FERNS: See section 2, "Houseplants".

Soil Ferns will grow in any good potting soil where cool root drainage is supplied by sand and milled sphagnum. Mix leafmold and garden loam in equal proportions. Some growers add finely-ground bark to their fern soil.

Certain ferns are, however, decidedly alkaline or acid in their soil preferences, and don't be deceived by the proximity of their original habitats: widely disparate soils exist in remarkably limited areas. The black-stemmed spleenwort and the walking fern, for example, are alkaline ferns that may give you trouble if planted in an overly acid mixture; contrariwise, the acid-loving rattlesnake fern won't thrive if your terrarium soil contains large amounts of limestone.

Food Ferns can be harmed by strong commercial fertilizers. Old-time fern growers kept their prized parlor specimens primed with diluted blood! It's available today as blood meal, a high-protein, nitrogenous fertilizer. Bone meal, slow-acting, safe and efficient, is also used.

FOAMFLOWER—*Tiarella cordifolia*

Attractive leaves and white flower spikes. This native wild plant works out well as background material in a larger terrarium. It's happiest, like most of it's kind, in partial shade.

GOLDTHREAD or YELLOWROOT—*Coptis trifolia*

This perennial plant of the buttercup family has evergreen leaves and a solitary white flower that makes it a natural focal feature; it can also be used as a filler. It requests both shade and moisture, and a peaty or sandy soil.

GROUND IVY—*Nepete hederacea*

This is a creeping plant of the mint family, with scallop-toothed leaves and tiny tubular purple flowers. Give it the partial shade it's used to.

HEPATICA AMERICANA, also called *Mayflower* and *Blue Anemone*

All of the hepaticas are charming little flowers, whose name suggests the liver-shaped leaves they grow. *H. americana* has the charm of being under 6 inches high. The Hepaticas (Liverleaf and Liverwort are alternate names) should be grown in rich woods soil, and shade.

JACK-IN-THE-PULPIT—*Arisaema* (ah-ri-see′ma) *triphyllum,* also called *Indian turnip*

This woodland favorite has two compound leaves. The spathe, or "pulpit" arches over the upright, club-shaped spadix, or spike. The overarching spathe is green and purple; the fruit consists of a mass of bright scarlet berries.

Plant ¾ -inch corms directly in, or in pots for transplanting to, the terrarium. Bulbs come in several sizes. The larger your corm, or bulb, the bigger your Jack will grow. A ¾ -inch corm will produce a plant 6 to 8 inches in height. It requires humus soil, shade, and moisture. It propagates easily by the division of its roots.

LICHEN (liken)

This dual form of plant life is at once algae and fungi, and manutures food as well as moisture. There are some 2,000 American lichens. Several of the coral and crust types are useful as fillers and as low foreground accent; their olive-green, greyish hue contrasts effectively with other more vivid terrarium greenery. For concealing the base of dried arrangements, use the crustlike lichen that grow on bark and on rocks, together with reindeer moss (*Cladonia rangiferina*), a grey, erect, tufted and multi-branched variety. Reindeer moss, even after it's been dried for years, becomes soft and pliant upon exposure to moisture.

Lichens usually grow on rocks as well as on the rough trunks of trees. They're a vital part of the intricate plan of growth and interdependence: they secrete acids that dissolve minerals, and so the rocky recesses where they reside are soon filled with plant life. An entire half-century may go into the creation of a single crustlike lichen rosette that spots the surface of a granite boulder. Look for reindeer moss in dry, acid woods and on barren rocky hilltops. Another variant, red-tipped and cupped, is found on old stumps and on rotten fence posts, but never in or near the polluted air of large cities.

LIVERLEAF, see *Hepatica*

MOSSES

As we've seen, the supporting role played by the mosses, *the* basic
terrarium plants, can't be overstressed: it's mosses for lining, patch-
ing, and filling. But, sealed into a miniature landscape, mosses of
varying browns and greens can become a showy feature planting as
well. Try using pincushion or broom moss, outlined with white pebbles, surrounded by fern and matlike species; use taller sphagnum as
background trees; low-key, but beautifully effective.

You can buy packaged decorator moss (used for hung baskets and
dried arrangements) that's entirely adequate for lining terrariums.
But live moss is much more attractive. In some form or other, it can
be found almost everywhere. It gives one pause to reflect that the
single forest floor of the Olympia Peninsula, in the Pacific Northwest,
is covered with more than *100 varieties* of moss! Known as either
rock or sheet moss, these verdant growths that carpet rocks, boulders
and decaying logs in swamps or deep woods make the best terrarium
liner you can find. But collect native mosses with care and restraint:
aside from their aesthetic contribution to the woodland scene, their
practical role is a substantial one; moss beds serve as spawning
ground for conifers and other seedlings, and in our era of vanishing
woodland, these moss beds are the sorely needed nurseries of tomor-
row.

The best and most congenial time for the gathering of moss and
lichen is when the weather's wet and so are they. You'll thrill at the
rain-washed sight of the mosses' plush and velvet-deep hues, a preview
of how they'll look inside of sealed glass. Even crusty lichens are
transformed by moisture from lifeless grey to a soft, vibrant olive
green. On wet moss-hunting days such as this, my footsteps muted
by the damp leaves, I frequently share the company of a deer or a
wildcat.

Although some mosses, such as the pincushion and broom species,
will grow in dryer locations, most varieties thrive in moist shade. The
sheet mosses, prime choice for lining glass container bottoms, sprawl
in luxurious mats over rocks, stumps, and decaying logs in their
natural habitat. Sphagnum grows in swampy bottomland. Don't pull
it up when it's frozen; its absorbent stems will be brittle and break like
glass.

The following varieties are native species; you can procure any and all of them in the woods, and some of them from terrarium suppliers.

SHEET MOSSES FOR TERRARIUM LINERS: *Brachythecium, Bryum bimum,* fern moss (*Thuidium delicatulum*).

MOSSES FOR FILLERS: Apple moss (*Bartramia pomiformis*), broom moss (*Dicranum scoparium*), furrowed moss (*Aulacomnium heterostichum*), pincushion moss (*Leucobryum glaucum*).

SPHAGNUM, comprising a large group of bog mosses, will grow, if undisturbed, in the same container for many years. Indispensable for packing roots, transplanting, and plant transportation, dried sphagnum leaves absorb 200 times their weight in water.

OXALIS, see *Wood Sorrel*

Partridgeberry

PARTRIDGEBERRY—*Mitchella repens*

Terrarium berry, one might dub this festive little vine that sprawls in 6- to 15-inch lengths. Tiny oval veined evergreen leaves and pinkish flowers are followed by the dual crimson drupes, containing many tiny nutlike seeds.

Even though it's annually harvested by the ton for brightening Christmas berry bowls, the doughty partridgeberry is holding its own, which is as gratifying as it is surprising. If you slit the berried cuttings with a scissors at the nodes, or branching joints, they'll root in moist terrarium moss, leaving the parent plant unscathed and fertile. My own partridgeberry source is a roadside patch that I share, not only with other glass garden buffs, but with the wild creatures for whose nourishment the colorful seed capsules were originally intended—and after a full decade of careful but plentiful picking, the patch is still not only productive but expanding at the margins.

Blossoms may appear anytime throughout the winter in the mild glass garden atmosphere. Use the short, berried lengths for foregrounds and central accent; plant longer pieces upright to lend color to a monotonous mass of back-of-the-bottle greenery.

If you buy partridgeberry from a florist or most other sources of plant supply, don't be alarmed when you're sold only the cuttings, with no roots. Partridgeberry is a wonderfully adaptable and vigorous plant; insert in your glass garden in moss, gravel and soil—and it will root almost immediately.

PIPSISSEWA—*Chimaphila* (ky-maf'illa)

C. maculata, the spotted pipsissewa, also called wintergreen or dragon's tooth, has white flowers in summer and pointed jagged leaves. *C. umbellata,* pipsissewa or prince's pine, is brilliant green, and grows pinkish-white fragrant flowers. Use it as background, or as a "tree" in a small landscape scene.

RATTLESNAKE PLANTAIN—*Goodyera pubescens,* also *Epipactis repens;* see "Orchids," section 2

Spotted pipsissewa

SOLOMON'S SEAL—*Polygonatum biflorum*

The graceful, tall, arching stems of this member of the lily family produce alternate leaves with yellow bell flowers at the axils. It is grown from horizontal surface roots; obviously, it's for use in more spacious gardens.

SPRING BEAUTY—*Claytonia virginica*

This plant is grown from fleshy tubers, has five-petaled pinkish flowers and linear succulent leaves. Some budded plants may be found beneath the forest leaves in winter. *C. virginica* grows from 4 to 6 inches high; it requires partial shade and a moist site.

Rattlesnake plantain

TRAILING ARBUTUS—*Epigea* (epi-jee'a) *repens.* Heath family

Each year, a few wildflower nurserymen offer limited supplies of this fragrant native with leathery evergreen leaves (brown-tipped in winter). As its name indicates (*Epigea* means "on the earth" in Greek), the arbutus is a creeping or ground plant. Some nurseries also sell budded cuttings for rooting in glass gardens, but orders must be placed with northern growers before the ground freezes. Here again, you can make your own stem cuttings: clip them in several-inch lengths in the early summer; wrap the ends tightly in wet shredded sphagnum; bury them in a mixture of sand and milled moss, and keep them in a shaded glass nursery. If you're the fortunate heir

169

to any surplus arbutus plants, pack them in moss, and store them in nursery terrariums. If there's enough light, subfreezing temperature won't hurt these hardy plants. On the contrary, it'll ensure their dormancy and survival.

Trailing arbutus is an acid sub-shrub, and has the same soil and preference for partial shade as the related mountain laurel (*E. repens* is also called ground laurel) and rhododendron. I fill arbutus bowls with decaying hemlock needles mixed with unenriched loam. If hemlock isn't available, mix old spruce needles or apple parings into the soil.

TRILLIUM NIVALE, also called *Dwarf Wakerobin*

A spectacular blossom consisting of 3-petaled flowers grown from tuberous rootstocks.

TWINFLOWER—*Linnaea borealis*

Woody trailing evergreen of the honeysuckle variety, with vines growing from 6- to 24-inch lengths supporting pink blossoms. This is a fine ground-covering plant. Give it good drainage in acid soil, and partial shade.

VIOLET—*Viola*

There are violets and more violets: hundreds of them, including many which are North American wildflowers. Most of the moisture-loving varieties are suitable for a cool terrarium.

Soil   Violets of most woodland varieties will flourish in leafmold of garden soils in which potatoes or vegetables are grown: add milled sphagnum to ensure proper drainage. Violets can be forced by the use of sod ground, as can violas; commercial growers resort to this expedient. But enriched soil tends to encourage stem and leaf, rather than flower, growth.

Care   Despite the saying that "the deeper the shade, the deeper the violet's purple," woodland violets do require light, but direct sunlight must either be filtered or supplied in weak doses. The purple tide of violet bloom in my Connecticut woodland is at its height about May 7, when the day-length averages about 14½ hours. The same light span, administered with artificial lighting (see chapter 5) will produce blossoms indoors.

Watering: It's important to duplicate moist spring growing conditions, but excessive moisture in the terrarium may cause stem and leaf rot. I advise frequent ventilation for drying, even though, conversely, these plants may need occasional watering.

As to temperature, they'll accept a wide thermometer range of from 60° to 70°; if exposed to undue heat, they'll become leggy.

V. priceana, or the Confederate violet, has large shiny leaves and mottled white-and-purple flowers. It combines well with *V. affinis* in showy blossom bowls. *V. blanda,* as its name suggests, is a small, sweet violet with tiny fragrant white flowers and leaves scaled down to go with them. Another fragrant violet is *V. odorata,* see "Garden Plants".

WILD GINGER—*Asarum* (ass'a-rum) *canadense*

Downy pairs of kidney-shaped leaves rise from the fragrant rootstocks. Chocolate-colored bell-like flowers hug the ground. You can buy them from a woodland nursery, and increase them easily by dividing the creeping rootstock. They need shade, a humus soil, and lots of moisture.

WINTERGREEN—*Gaultheria procumbens,* also called *Checkerberry, Teaberry, Ground Holly,* and *Spice Berry.* Heath family

This is the common wintergreen of our dry woods. Its shining aromatic leaves grow on trailing stems with red edible berries. Although it's a hardy plant, it does not transplant easily; better to get it potted, and propagate from cuttings of half-ripened wood. The trailing underground roots can be wound around circular or square planters of some dimensions. It requires a decidedly acid soil, and partial shade.

WOOD SORREL—*Oxalis*

This is an accent plant whose clover-like leaves fold at night, or in dark weather. I'll list some of the varieties most popular for terrarium use. *O. cernua* is known as the Bermuda buttercup although neither a buttercup nor originally from Bermuda (where, however, it was naturalized). As you'd guess, it has yellow flowers. *O. deppei,* with red-purple blooms, is nicely scaled for terrarium use, growing to 4-8 inches. *O. lasiandra* has clusters of pink flowers on sprawling stems that grow as long as 18 inches; it needs plenty of room. *O. martiana* has handsome, variegated foliage and rose-colored blooms. *O. montana* has dainty purple-veined flowers of white or pale pink; finally, there is *O. rubra,* an old-fashioned kitchen-window plant whose flowers range the pink-rose spectrum. They're generally grown from bulbs or from roots and put into the terrarium as small plants.

YELLOWROOT, see *Goldthread*

Sources of Supply

MATERIALS (Numbers refer to Suppliers, part 2)

CONTAINERS

Crystalite Indoor Greenhouse, 22
Hotkaps, 3
In-the-Row Plastic Greenhouse, 22
Miniature Greenhouses, 1, 3, 23
Plantariums, 5
Swedish Crystal Easter Eggs, 13
Terrariums, 1, 23

SOIL, MOSS, AND PLANTING MEDIUMS

Cacti-Succulent Soil, 14
Moss, Dried Decorator, 16
Moss, Live: sphagnum, swamp mosses and living sheet moss for lining
   terrariums; also fungi and lichens, 1
Orchid-growing Media (osmundine fiber, fir bark), 22
Sphagnum, Milled and Unmilled: "Sure-Fire Sowing and Growing
   Mix," 22
Terrarium Planting Medium, 1

STONES, LANDSCAPING EFFECTS, ORNAMENTS

Featherock (stone), 6

Florist charcoal, 1
Maine Driftwood, 1
Terrarium Figurines, 1

PLANTING ACCESSORIES

Flexible Mechanical Finger, 32
Gro-lamps and Tubes, 3, 22
Heating Cables, 22
Plastic Plant Trays; Fiber Pots; "Jiffy-7" Pelleted Pots; 3, 22
Seed Sower; Soil Thermometer; 22
Sprayers and Sprinklers
   Brass "Mist-Ifier," 3, 22
   Rubber Hand Sprinkler, 3, 22
   SYONeX Plastic Hand Sprayer, 1, 23

PLANTS

African Violets, Miniature and Semi-Miniature; 2
Arbutus
   Plants; Unrooted Budded Cuttings; 1
   Potted, 7, 17, 26
Aquatic Plants, including Miniature Indoor Water Lilies, 31
Cacti and Succulent Plants and Seed, 10, 14; Seed, 22, 28
Carnivorous Plants: See "Insectivorous Plants" below.
Crocus sieberi Bulbs, 12, 33
Ferns, 1, 7, 17, 19, 21, 26, 30; Seed, 21
Fernarium, complete with spores, growing container, sterile planting
   medium and instructions, 1
Forsythia and Pussy Willow Cuttings, 18
Gloxinias, 2; Seed, 2, 22
Insectivorous Plants, 1, 23
   Catalog with pertinent facts on growing insectivores, 23
   Darlington Cobra Orchid Seed, 22
   Venus's Fly Trap, Ready-to-grow, in covered plastic container, 24
Lily-of-the-Valley Pips for Indoor Forcing, 22, 27
Miniature Trees, 8, 20, 23, 36
Mosses, see above.
Mushrooms

Spawn, 3
Ready-to-grow spawn in container, needing only water to grow;
6 x 8. Also Mushroom Farm, larger size, 15
Orchids, Tropical, 11, 22; Seed Starting Kit, 22
Oxalis, 22
Pachysandra (*terminalis*), 3, 22, 32
Partridgeberry, 1; Plants available most wild flower nurseries
Peppergrass (Curlycress), 3
Primrose, 31
Silveredge, 23, 33
Violas (Johnny Jump-Ups), 33, 34; Seed, 22
Woodland Plants for Terrariums, 1 and other nurseries listed

SEEDS

African Violet, Begonia, Palm, Coffea Arabica, Cyperus, and many
other foliage and flowering plants suitable for growing in glass gardens, 22
Conifer Tree Seeds, 8, 22
Ornamental Grass and Everlasting Seed for Dried Arrangements,
3, 22

MISCELLANEOUS

Flower-Dri, Silica Gel Drying Compound for Preserving Flowers;
3, 25
Turtles, 31

Part 2

1. Arthur Eames Allgrove
   North Wilmington, Massachusetts 01877
2. Albert H. Buell
   Eastford, Connecticut
3. W. Atlee Burpee Co.
   Hunting Park Avenue at 18th Street
   Philadelphia, Pennsylvania 19132
4. Capitola Violet Garden
   3640 Gross Road
   Santa Cruz, California

5. Emerson Industries, Inc.
   Hempstead, New York

6. Featherock, Inc.
   6331 Hollywood Boulevard
   Los Angeles 28, California

7. Gardens of the Blue Ridge
   Ashford, North Carolina

8. Girard Nurseries
   Geneva, Ohio 44041

9. Grillet's Nature Novelties
   Route 2, Box 340
   Palmyra, Pennsylvania 17078

10. Henrietta's Nursery
    1345 North Brawley
    Fresno, California 93705

11. International Growers Exchange
    P. O. Box 397
    Farmington, Michigan 48024

12. P. de Jager & Sons, Inc.
    South Hamilton, Massachusetts 01982

13. Georg Jensen
    667 Fifth Avenue
    New York 10022

14. Johnson Cactus Gardens
    Paramount, California

15. Lakeland Nurseries Sales
    Hanover, Pennsylvania 17331

16. Larchfield Products, Inc.
    Manhattan-Pacific Building
    Stamford, Connecticut 16902

17. Leslie's Wild Flower Nurseries
    30 Summer Street
    Methuen, Massachusetts 01844

18. Michigan Bulb Company
    Dept. Dy-713
    Grand Rapids, Michigan 49502

19. Eugene Mincemoyer
    Route 2, Box 482
    New Prospect Road
    Jackson, New Jersey
20. Musser Forests, Inc.
    Box 738
    Indiana, Pennsylvania 15701
21. Orchid Gardens
    Route 1, Box 441
    Grand Rapids, Minnesota 55744
22. George W. Park Seed Co., Inc.
    Greenwood, South Carolina 29646
23. Peter Pauls Nurseries
    Canandaigua, New York 14424
24. Plant Oddities
    Box 127
    Basking Ridge, New Jersey 07920
25. Plantabs Corporation
    1101 Maryland Avenue
    Baltimore, Maryland
26. Putney Nursery
    Putney, Vermont
27. John Scheepers, Inc.
    (Specialists, Flower Bulbs)
    63 Wall Street
    New York, N.Y. 10005
28. R. H. Shumway
    Dept. 348
    Rockford, Illinois
29. Rube Sneller, the Mushroom Feller
    Chesterland, Ohio
30. The Three Laurels
    Route 3, Box 15
    Marshall, North Carolina
31. Three Springs Fisheries, Inc.
    Lilypons, Maryland 21717

32. Ullman Devices Corporation
    P.O. Box 398
    Ridgefield, Connecticut
33. Wayside Gardens
    Mentor, Ohio
34. White Flower Farm
    Litchfield, Connecticut 06759
35. Woodland Acres Nursery
    Route 2
    Crivitz, Wisconsin 54114
36. Yoshimura Bonsai Company, Inc.
    Tarrytown, New York

Index

Credits and Acknowledgements

Photos (except where otherwise noted) by Robert Dickstein and the author

Photos on pages 37, 40 and 71 courtesy of Grillet's Nature Novelties

Plantings in photos on pages 12 and 27 by Marc Meyer Jr., Nosegay-at-the-Carlyle Shop, New York

Quintet bauble on page 12, and glass egg (Color Plate I), by Morgantown Glass Guild

Glamour Blue Crystal, candle lamps with lustres, and tripod (Color Plates III, IV and V), by Fostoria Glass Company

Plantarium on page 80 courtesy of Emerson Industries

Settings for color plates in the home of Mr. George Anders

Drawings by Barbara Shapira

Planting Records